"Chin Up, Head Down"

Contents

Dedication

For
Rob, Zac, and Steely
In Loving Memory of Cyrus
Celer et Audax

Acknowledgements

I would like to thank Steve Rider for giving me the confidence in how I write, which has resulted in being able to tell my story. Also to Helena Drysdale, via The Writers Workshop, for her guidance which has been paramount. A special thanks to Robin Thatcher, Cyrus's father for his huge input and total support without which I don't think I could have completed this on my own, and finally to Jon Cooksey for his introduction to Ryan Gearing at FireStep Publishing.

CHAPTER 1

TWO MEN

I watched the mosquito land and test my skin for the right place to push its hypodermic proboscis through the tough outer layer and so start the process of letting my blood. It flew off bloated. I was aware of the bite on my ankle but knew that it would never itch. I was numb: it didn't matter. Only hours before, my life had been shattered in an instant.

It was four o'clock on the first morning of my new life – a life I had not really planned for or wanted any part of. My feet were wet from crossing the grass to sit by the pond, where I looked blindly at the lilies. The warm air was heavy with the scent of the remnants of night, and filled with birds finding their voices in the dawn and the faint whine of the now distant mosquito. My new life. How do I begin to live it? I was more than happy with the old one.

Grief is physical. I had never known that – well, why should I? It had never been part of my life. It's like a gaping hole, deep and dark, filled with burning pains that reach up from your toes, strangling everything as they creep upwards to turn around and start back down again on their constant journey, never stopping or pausing to rest. Like the ebb and flow of the ocean – my ocean – awash with the flotsam and jetsam of pain and torment. I thought I might be sick, but that would have been a relief – so I wasn't. I was burning from the inside out, and even my tears dried as they fell on my cheeks.

Had I always known this day would come? No. I had just hoped against hope that it wouldn't. How could he be dead? This was not supposed to happen to my family. It was something that you heard on the news or read about in the paper – something that happened to other families – not mine. I had been as guilty as the rest, of flicking the channel or turning the page because it wasn't my family – it wasn't personal. It is now, and here I am in the middle of this sea of grief and pain, and it is real.

Parallel lines – like railway tracks that run all over the world; the world in my head running along lines that go nowhere, never stopping, never ending. Just parallel to Rob's, Zac's and Steely's, sometimes crossing, but never meeting completely. Perhaps that is what grief and pain really are; a line that runs its course through our lives, driving us forward but not showing us what is at the end – or if there is an end. There was a beginning though, that is a fact.

There were two of them. Men in suits, wearing ties. I knew. I was opening the window before going to bed – it was 10.20 pm on Tuesday 2nd June, 2009. The night that my life, as I knew it, finished.

Looking out, I wondered who they were and what they were doing. It was during the local elections and for a split second I thought it might be candidates touting for business – but who would be coming up the drive at this time of night? I knew. They reached the door and Rob, grabbing his glasses, ran downstairs, opened it before they could knock. 'Mr Thatcher?' They held out their identity cards, but they didn't have to – I knew. 'Is there somewhere we can come in and we can all sit down?' I knew. 'Just tell me it's not the worst,' Rob pleaded. Surely he had been wounded and they needed to get us to the hospital? Yes, that must be it, but why would they ask us to sit? I knew. I stood there in my 'Winnie the Pooh' nightie as they uttered the words that would be any parent's worst nightmare.

I shouted up the stairs for Steely. He came down looking sheepish, thinking I was going to tell him off for not putting his plate in the dishwasher again. He looked at me and laughed as I put my hand to my mouth and whispered, 'He's been killed.' 'You're having a laugh,' he replied. Then he looked at my face and paled. Rob went to the garage to get Zac. 'Zac, mate, you need to come in, it's the worst possible thing.'. Zac and Sharpie, his friend, came to the back door and saw the men. 'Cyrus was killed this morning,' Rob said.

Sharpie said, 'I'll go.' What else could he do? They asked us to sit. How do you sit when someone has just stabbed you in the heart? I refused. I was not going to sit while they gave us brief details about how our son Cyrus had been killed by an IED in Afghanistan at 9.15 this morning. Which morning? Our morning or their morning? How many hours difference were there; were they in front or behind? Had he been dead all day and we'd not known?

I'll never forget that man's face. What a shitty job, telling people they've lost a son, thousands of miles from home, in a dusty land we'll never visit or even care about. What were the details, when would we know, when would we want to know? All sound was muffled. All I could see was my ruined family and feel a blind panic. Nothing will ever been the same again, oh God.

I think that's when I was first aware of the feeling of walking through glue. Sticky, smothering, exhausting, so little sound and light gets through. It is all diffused and the glue is slowly strangling us, bearing down, hateful – a weighted mist of glue and grief and pain. Oh, the pain.

That was five and a half weeks ago. So much has happened. Most of it in a blur, a dream – a glue-filled life of haunting memories.

They were so sad, those two men, with pain behind their eyes. They referred to their notes, unable to keep eye contact. How do you tell people such awful news and it not kill some small part of you? After they left – I don't know how long they stayed – the glue descended. I think we were given a name, someone who would come and see us, look after us, guide us.

That someone was WO II Ian Tindall of 7 Rifles, based at Brock Barracks here in Reading – our Visiting Officer. He has been our source of information throughout this awful journey, the bearer of both good and bad news, utterly reliable and compassionate, making this whole process as smooth and painless as he can. It must be hard to watch people grieve.

A new world opened up, one of which we had never really been a part. We were introduced to the ranks, what all the letters stood for, in what order everyone fitted together to make up a battalion. What a Warrant Officer II was, and why was he our Visiting Officer. Simply, a Warrant Officer holds a Warrant from the Queen. Class I is the Regimental Sergeant Major, one per battalion – Class II is one rank lower, and there can be up to ten per battalion. These Warrant Officers have been promoted through the ranks rather than being a Commissioned Officer, who holds the Queen's Commission and usually come out of Sandhurst.

Visiting Officers are volunteered by the Regiment, and when Ian first arrived he came with a little black notebook containing our names and address, Cyrus's date and place of death. He took out his pen and waited. That little book was obviously going to fill over the months, it would become his method of ensuring no question went unanswered and all information was relayed.

This was a world that Cyrus was a part of and loved. I can see why now, five and a half weeks later. I always knew though. It was just him – a life he loved no more or less than he loved us, but a life to which he was suited – a life that made him a man. He had entered the realm of 'a band of brothers'; men who would lay down their lives for each other, and now he had done just that – he had laid down his life.

The Army said they would not release his name until we were ready. I will never be ready. We asked for twenty-four hours. There were so many people we needed to tell. That awful sound of the phone ringing, and when it's picked up the other end you have to say the words that have changed our life, and will now change theirs. 'Hello' is impossible; how do you go on to say, 'He was killed this morning'? It sticks in your throat, choking you. Sobbing, the words don't really come out, but they know, the people on the other end of the line. They know.

Glue. Or is it pain? So many phone calls to make, always starting with that impossible 'Hello', always ending with whispered words that shatter, and make others scream. We couldn't get hold of my mother or Rob's dad – where the hell were they? We needed to tell them before it was all over the news. Frustration was added now. It wasn't until the Thursday morning we eventually made contact, thirty-six hours after we had been told, just as the first news bulletins went out.

I haven't screamed, and I wonder why, when I told some people, they did. He didn't belong to them. He was ours. It is not their right to scream and drop the phone. That right is ours, and we haven't screamed yet – so what makes them think they can? Their screams make it so much more difficult, because I have to tell them to calm down, tell them it's ok, tell them the scant details that I know. Why am I having to comfort them? I know why – because I've had to hurt them by telling them, but it doesn't make it any easier to have to pick up the phone and tell the next person. I wish they hadn't screamed. I could feel my patience snap. My patience, my heart, my soul.

In this world of mobile phones, the internet and text messages you know that within an hour the news will have spread. We've had to wake some people because it's getting close to midnight. Oh God, all those people whom we have to inject with pain. They have never known this pain, and neither have we. It is all so new, so crushing – so sad. Maybe the glue is really sadness. It has been so much harder to tell Cyrus's friends than it was to tell my own mother. I guess that is another story, even though it is interwoven with this one. I feel she has no right to grieve. You should only have the right to grieve for those you have known, but since this happened I have grieved for many other mothers, fathers, brothers and sisters. There have been so many since, so many more to come… so much glue and tears. So many families broken, marriages over, siblings split and so many more to follow, and so many that went before.

Grief is selfish. Only I really know how I feel. I can run that parallel line with Rob and the boys, but only they know how they grieve. Windows and seats on a train, each of us pointing in the same direction, just sitting in different places, seeing different scenes pass by. A friend of mine helped me to see it like that. She was so right. Different seats and different scenes – same journey, equal pain, equal sadness.

Grief is lonely. It is selfish, lonely and all consuming. It attacks you when you least expect it. I admit that I have had whole hours when I've not thought about Cyrus. Should I feel guilty about that? A whole hour – or maybe it was just five minutes – but it felt like an hour. I've lost all sense of time. I am not even sure what the day is, and have no idea of the date. I find it hard to remember how long it has been since those two men in suits crunched their way up our gravel drive to shatter our world. How many weeks since the funeral? I've no idea. Does that make me a bad person, a terrible uncaring mother? Should I remember these significant dates and days, or is this the way my brain is helping me to cope? I'm sure I would go mad – perhaps I am already there. My reality does not seem to match anyone else's. Glue has taken all sense away and replaced it with sadness. My reality is no longer there. I know in my heart that this will change slowly, but swimming against this sea of glue is so hard, I'm exhausted all the time. Everything is an effort.

Breathing. I am still breathing and I cannot stop it. I cannot stop my heart from beating, pushing me forward, making me go on. My heart is broken but it still keeps beating, my lungs inflate and deflate. I cannot prevent it. Is there a purpose? Do I still have a job to do? Yes. I have a family that needs me as much as I need them. I need to see their faces, hear their voices, share their lives – even though the glue makes them harder to see at times. They have dreams too, and I will still be there to help them fulfil them if I can.

He was a school refuser, my son the soldier. He hated the classroom, felt inadequate because his reading was slower than others' – but he was bright and that frustrated him too. He didn't know what he was going to do with his life. 'What will I do Mum?' he used to ask. We would spend many an hour on the sofa cuddling and talking, me trying to soothe and placate my confused, angry and sometimes misunderstood son, so like his dad, he too a school refuser and equally difficult and angry at that age.

I have seen first hand, through hard work and determination, Rob's achievements – what many in his past would not have thought possible. He has a successful general building business, employing many over the years, that has given us, as a family, a full and happy life. The boys idolised him, so how could I encourage without comparing?

Moments when I would try to hold Cyrus's long, lean fingers still, stopping him from biting his nails or digging them into the palms of his hands; tracing the freckles across the bridge of his straight, slim nose; soothing his mood, whispering words of encouragement and love, telling him there was a place in the world for him, and that he would be successful one day. I don't think he really believed me until he decided to join the Army.

There were other people along the way who helped him – the recruiting officer who saw the potential, teachers and assistants who knew he had it in him and helped him to believe in himself. Once he decided to join up, his own personal army arrived in different forms and helped him achieve what he had once thought impossible. We were so proud of him during those last few months at school. Who would have thought that he would have done so well? He certainly knew what he wanted and did everything in his power to get it. Thank you to those who shared that part of his journey. I will forever be indebted to you. You know who you are and I do not need to name you.

'Even those who do not go to university can achieve greatness and honours,' Rob said to my mother on the day of the funeral. She seems to think that you can only attain greatness through education, but we are all different, and some of us can achieve it in other ways. My children are those sorts of people. People who live their lives to the best of their ability, collecting friends and experiences along the way, not needing books or paper certificates to tell them that they are successful.

My children are people who have hearts larger than life, and who touch others without even knowing they are doing it, changing their lives forever, for the better. My boys, my pride, my loves, my children, my men.

They have picked us up and carried us on this path, the Army. People coming and going, cards, letters, flowers. I do not want any of them. I want him back. The house smells of lilies and pain. Cards flutter to the floor every morning and we go through the ritual of reading them, amazed at how many there are. Some from people who we have not heard from for years, and some from people we do not know – people swimming in glue like us. We are not the first or the last. So many people, so many words, so much pain and sadness. All I want is him back. People mean well, but they cannot help – not yet. It is all still too raw and open, too selfish.

CHAPTER 2

REPATRIATION

I will never forget Lyneham. That was not how he was supposed to come home. Not in a coffin on an enormous aircraft filled with silent men and death.

He was not alone; there were two other soldiers, Lance Corporal Nigel Moffat, the Light Dragoons, and Corporal Stephen Bolger of 1st Battalion, the Parachute Regiment. Two other families who were numb like us.

One of the questions those men in suits asked was whether we would like Cyrus to be flown home on Friday 5th June or the following Tuesday. Why would we want to wait? He needed to be home – we needed him home. I couldn't bear the thought of him lying dead, thousands of miles away. No we wanted him home as soon as possible.

Apparently the repatriation had to be within ten days. The delay is because an MOD-sponsored mortician has to fly to theatre (Afghanistan) to prepare the bodies; there are only five C-17's available to carry coffins, and theatre wished to organise a ramp/sunset ceremony. Families are scattered all over the world and I guess they need several dates for bringing them home, so that the families can get to RAF Lyneham, Wiltshire.

Ian collected us on Thursday and took us to the Hilton Hotel, Swindon, where we were to stay the night. The repatriation is a military ceremony that the families are invited to attend, and because of the formalities of the day they need to make sure all who wish to attend are in place the night before. A maximum of seven close family/friends are funded from the public purse. Just the four of us went to meet him ... watch him come home.

We were met at the hotel by Major Mark Owen, the Quartermaster, also Officer Commanding Rear Operations in Ballykinler, Northern Ireland, where 2 Rifles is based; he would speak on behalf of the Rifles at Cyrus's funeral. We also met Captain Richard Sellars, Regimental Administration Officer of 2 Rifles, who held the Regiment's purse strings and coordinated all the funeral arrangements.

They explained to us briefly what would happen the next day at Lyneham – that we would meet the coroner in the morning, who would talk us through their procedures. It was too much to take in and I felt exhausted.

That night, while we waited for Cyrus to come home, Steely ordered broccoli and stilton soup. Strange – he doesn't even like stilton. He just needed to order something and that was what he saw on the menu. I don't remember what I ordered; I only know it was taken away untouched.

We sat staring, unseeing, at our plates, while the plane of death rumbled high above the clouds, bringing our soldier son home. We were all so sad and heavy with the weight of the unknown. It was all Zac could do to talk, but he did – through clenched teeth, shoulders hunched, his face drawn and pale. I don't think he even looked up through his shaggy fair hair to made eye contact. It's not a matter of being rude or ignorant, because none of our children are; it's that everything seemed so impossible. Looking directly at someone might have made it true, and we all secretly so hoped it wasn't. We learnt to paint our masks on that night – a guise we still use, anything to make it seem normal. But nothing is normal – not any more.

The morning brought more officials the MOD-appointed undertaker (Kenyon Repatriation Ltd), and a representative from the Wiltshire Coroner's Office and Air Force personnel, as the ceremony takes place on an RAF base, and they needed to brief us on air issues and the RAF's involvement in the day.

We sat in a semi-circle, the other families in their own ones, and the coroner came to us individually and explained in a hushed voice what the procedure was going to be. He had been given the initial report from the medical staff in Camp Bastion, Afghanistan, which he had read. He didn't give us any details, only that they needed to do a DNA test; I guess as he was a blast victim they had to make sure which bits were his. Surely not my baby, not in pieces, not needing to be identified by genes and chromosomes. What about his face? Could he not be identified by that? There was information, but no information. I didn't hear what I needed to know. Had it been instantaneous? Please tell me he didn't suffer, that he knew nothing of what had happened – but he couldn't say. No help to me, then. He then said that they would take him to the Radcliffe in Oxford for an autopsy processing before he was passed on to the Berkshire Coroner and finally the funeral directors. 'Processing' – what the hell does that mean? This can't be happening, it's all too macabre and unreal. Can we see him? That seems to be the burning question, but he doesn't know because he hasn't seen the body, and he doesn't know what condition he is in. Condition? Oh God what does that mean? So many questions but none answered. Frustration takes over then – frustration at my inability to process the information. I don't want to be here – this can't be my life now. We are all numb, silent and numb, as there is nothing to say.

As we were driven through the gates at Lyneham, everyone we passed saluted – how odd. They didn't know us, didn't know Cyrus – they just stood there silently, saluting as we drove on. It felt as if we were the honoured ones. I wasn't sure how to react to their sorrow and pride. It was so moving, then the enormity of it hit. There in front of us was the runway, huge, empty, and waiting. He would be landing there soon. How do I bear this? Hands clenched and mouth dry.

We appeared to be the last to arrive. The other two shattered families were sitting quietly, waiting. Waiting for instructions; none of us knew what to do; waiting for pain, waiting – just waiting.

Handshakes with uniforms – so many medals, so many ranks, so many sad and sorry eyes. Lieutenant General Nick Parker, CBE, Colonel Commandant, The Rifles, was the Chief of the General Staff's representative, and as such was also the main VIP who took the parade (he was awarded the Knight Commander of the Order of Bath in the Birthday Honours a few weeks after the repatriation and became Lieutenant General Sir Nick Parker, KCB, CBE). He apologised for the formality of the procedures but explained that it is just 'what the Army do – all this pomp and ceremony'. 'Cyrus would have appreciated it,' I said. He loved that part – all the uniforms, the total package of being a unit of order and history – just as much as the soldiering. I'm not sure that it wasn't all completely lost on me.

They were so kind, those men – Lieutenant General Nick Parker, Major Mark Owen, Captain Richard Sellars – explaining about the order in which the coffins would come out of the plane. It isn't by rank of the fallen but regimental seniority, and so Cyrus as a Rifleman was to be last. It didn't dawn on me the implication of that, until we were on the tarmac. The padre moved silently, brushing against us with his words of sorrow and comfort. There are no words of comfort, not when nothing will ever comfort again.

Then we were there standing in the rain, not moving, just looking for the plane that was carrying death.

The uniforms were there, standing in front of the marquees, saluting, both Army and Air Force, too many names and ranks to remember – too much glue anyway. They told us to look left towards the clock tower; that was where we would first catch sight of the plane. The sky was dark grey and we stood there, chairs touching the backs of our legs. 'We're going to stand for him and be proud,' Rob said, so together we did. The marquees fluttered in the breeze, it was cold and damp – typical June weather.

The aircraft was so long in coming; the uniforms still saluting. Eventually we could see three white lights in the distance and a bell started to toll, then the plane was flying past so slowly I thought it would drop there on the runway right in front of us. There was no air. Perhaps we were all holding our breath. Then he was home. The force of the feeling was physical. He was home – but not the way he was supposed to be.

Because of the geography of the airfield, it wasn't possible to watch the aircraft land, so after the flypast we were taken back into the terminal building to watch via CCTV screens. We then had to wait for the Air Force to clear the plane of any defence systems, and carry out safety checks, which took about an hour.

RAF catering staff provided food for us, but the smell made me feel so sick I asked if it could be taken away. What on earth made them think we'd be able to eat at a time like this? Lieutenant General Nick Parker came and sat with us. He was covered in medals and he had the largest hands I've ever seen. What a nice man – what a disgusting way to have to meet him. We talked in whispers – there were the other families too, looking as lost and confused as we were, talking to the other battalions' representatives.

The padre moved between the families and recited each regiment's collect – a short prayer. I wasn't aware of hearing the other ones, only the Rifles':

> *O Almighty God, the sure stronghold of each succeeding age, guard us your servants of The Rifles, that we may uphold and be worthy of the great traditions of our former Regiments; and as we were chosen to be swift and bold, may we seek with courage your grace in every time of need,*

> *and so be patient and persevere in running the*
> *race that is set before us, as did your Son Jesus*
> *Christ our Lord. Amen.*

It's the 'swift and bold' (often written in its Latin form *Celer et Audax*) that makes me choke. It describes Riflemen so well. 'Fearless' perhaps should be in there somewhere – I'm sure they do have fear, but take it all in their stride, going with the flow of their job and what it means to be a soldier.

Eventually they called us outside again. To stand so close to that plane was almost frightening. These aircraft are enormous and I felt small. The back was open and the first Bearer Party moved up the ramp and disappeared into the plane. It seemed an age before they were back in sight, bearing the first coffin. Twice we watched as each of the regiments' Bearer Parties moved on to and out of the plane: then it was Cyrus. Moving backwards, Serjeant Major Lee Jones directed them down towards the tarmac to the sound of *The Last Post*. There was no air – how can I breathe? How can this coffin that's draped in a flag have someone so dear inside? How can he be dead?

They walked so slowly, so precisely, with such pride and sadness. Those men with their shiny boots and solemn faces, carefully carrying his coffin to the waiting hearse. There was no other noise that I remember – only the rain and the bugle sounding Reveille as the wheels of the hearse started to move off towards the Chapel of Rest. It was the first time we'd heard those bugles in context and my blood turned to ice, every hair on my body stood up, goose pimples ran across my skin and

aunting is the only way I can describe it
yed with such passion, projecting such
s to call to arms, notes to say goodbye, notes
I'd never had to hear. It is their final farewell, and
symbolises that the duty of the dead is over and they
can rest in peace. It is impossible to control the lump in
your throat and the tears that follow.

We met them – the Bearer Party – inside, away from
the runway and the plane of death. What could we say?
None of us knew where to look. No one could bear to
look into our eyes, and I couldn't bear to look into theirs.
How many more of these awful days will they have to go
through? They volunteer to do this – amazing.

After a long embarrassing silence, T, one of the of
bearer party, decided to recount a story of when he
and Cyrus were in Kosovo as part of a Peace-Keeping
Force, leading up to and during their national elections.
They had been tasked with protecting monasteries and
churches, and on this particular day a wedding was
taking place. Apparently Cyrus – 'Thatch' – decided
to make himself scarce. The next thing they knew, on
the top steps of the church, right in the middle of the
wedding party, was Thatch with his cheeky grin, posing
for the family photos. T said he would miss him, as he
was the morale of the platoon, the one who always had a
smile, a giggle, and a kind word, the one who was always
'up for it' – the one who had so much more to give and
live for.

While we waited for the coffins to be taken to the
Chapel of Rest, I found I was beginning to feel light-
headed, and they kindly brought back the plates of food
I'd sent away earlier. We all had a small sandwich, which

helped take away some of the nausea. One of the Royal Air Force personnel came and asked us if we'd like to go and look inside the plane. As we walked towards it, the sheer size became apparent. I'd expected it to be empty, but as we walked up the rear ramp we saw that the whole crew were there, standing to attention. It was so unexpected, them saluting – again that feeling of everything being surreal, people saluting us and we were not even in the Army. We shook their hands and thanked them for looking after Cyrus on the way home. They smiled sadly and said that it was an honour, the least they could do, and told us that each of the boys had been accompanied by someone the whole journey, sitting with the coffin, making sure that they are not left on their own at any stage. Strange how you don't think along those lines as a civilian, the services criss-cross and help each other in ways I'd not really considered. It was humbling and very comforting to think that he'd not been on his own inside that huge hollow, draughty space filled with strapping and clamps, metal seats running along the fuselage – not a comfortable place to spend hour upon noisy hour, flying in the plane of death. Perhaps that's just a 'mother' thing, comforting, knowing he had not been left alone. It is also because his body was effectively 'a crime scene', as he had been unlawfully killed.

It was now approaching twenty hours since we'd left home, every hour getting worse, leading us towards the moment when we would be with him again. Dread fills each segment of time. We have no idea what to expect, and don't know how we'll react. Will my knees buckle? Will I die myself?

An RAF car took us to the Chapel of Rest. It was quiet and surrounded by flowers, and the padre was waiting outside, in case we needed him. Thoughtful, but I only needed one thing and he couldn't perform that miracle. It smelt of new wood. There were several doors, one for each family, one for each hero, one for each agony. We were shown into a small room and there it was – his Union Flag-draped coffin. I touched it, and it was cold. We ran our hands over it, trying to get a feel of him through the wood and fabric. I lay my head where I guessed his chest would be. Where was he? I knew he was home but I couldn't feel him. How do we go on?

Zac stood rolling a cigarette; stupidly I said, 'You can't smoke in here.' Of course he wasn't going to smoke, what was I thinking? He just looked at me and kept on rolling. He placed the completed cigarette on the coffin, together with a yellow clipper lighter. 'One for the road, mate,' he whispered.

Who knows how long we were there, touching the coffin? We read the prayer that had been left in leaflets with a red cross on the front. Soothing words of a religion I don't have or understand. His name was in them so we took them. They were ours.

The car was waiting outside to take us back to the hangar. All I wanted was to go home, but Ian explained we had to stay here at Lyneham while the cortege was driven through the village of Wootton Bassett, where an informal public ceremony is held every time one of our fallen men or women comes home. The whole town centre stops: shopkeepers, the general public, service personnel, friends and relatives come together standing on the pavements lining the main street, weeping as the cortege slowly makes its way through. A bell tolls and everything falls silent, flowers are thrown, the British Legion in its finery stands to attention, Standard Bearers proudly salute and lay down their Standards. Changes not long after Cyrus's repatriation mean that any family members present at RAF Lyneham are now taken ahead of the cortege to stand and wait in Wootton Bassett town centre by the Memorial, where the hearse comes to a brief stop. We didn't do that – we had to wait at the air base until the town's streets had cleared of mourners. Our cerem ony was a private one at RAF Lyneham; the public one is in Wootton Bassett.

Later that evening we learned that several of Zac's and Cyrus's friends had joined the mourners at Wootton Bassett and had stood in the crowd at the side of the main road waiting, wondering which of the three hearses his coffin would be in. When they saw the yellow clipper lighter on the coffin in the last hearse they knew. I'm so glad that Zac did that – it was a marker in more ways than one. How lovely of them to make the journey down the motorway, perhaps they too had to make sure it was real and not a mistake.

The final part of an exhausting day awaited us. As we got into the car, Ian handed us a manila envelope. At some stage we'd been asked, although I've no idea by whom, if there were any personal items of Cyrus's that we would like to come back with his body. We had asked for his camera and i-Pod. We opened the envelope and along with his IiPod and camera was a free-post airmail letter used by the forces known as a bluey, from Stewart Elliott who was still out in Afghanistan.

Stewart and Cyrus had become best friends, a friendship that began when Cyrus was posted to Northern Ireland in January 2008. We only knew Stewart as Elliott, the reason being that within the Army first names rarely apply – Cyrus was known as Thatch. Over a period of time we were to hear of Youngy, Willo, Fun Time, Tommo, Moni, Smudge, Mad Dog, Marshy, Stracs, Malou, Reedy, Mac, Vaughny, Joe and G.

In his letter, Elliott wrote that he and Cyrus had made a promise to each other, that should anything happen they would let the other one's family know that they had left a letter that was only to be read in the event of their death. In Elliott's letter he said that Cyrus had told him it was hidden on the top of our kitchen units.

I don't really remember the drive home. I think the boys slept. I could not. It didn't seem right that I should sleep – have the pleasure of forgetting for a few minutes. Sleep is both a relief and guilt. It has become easier, but the nightmares still trickle in night after night, stealing into the corners that I thought I'd kept safe – corners that I thought no one could see, or fit into. They are my corners, but then they are my dreams, so I guess they go hand in hand. My nightmares are like a movie, and they come with their own soundtrack. I wish I could turn the sound down and switch the movie off.

CHAPTER 3

LIEUTENANT PAUL MERVIS

Back at home, too exhausted to think but strangely elated because Elliott had told us that Cyrus had written to us. Rob spent ages looking in, on and under the kitchen cupboards, but he couldn't find the letter. It was so disappointing – we were desperate to find it, thinking that it might make us feel better somehow, or at least give us a chance to be close to him again through his words.

The next day, Saturday, Rob and I went down to Glastonbury to see his dad and step-mother. Rob is the middle of five children, and when he was ten his parents divorced. Rob chose to live with his dad. His relationship with his mother and siblings never really recovered from this split and they now have little contact.

There is a strange sense of duty that comes from both Rob and his dad that, to me, is sometimes hard to fathom. They have an unusual relationship in that, as a child and teenager, Rob was left to his own devices with little or no direction from his father. At one stage Social Services were alerted to this situation, and there was the threat of Rob being taken into care. During several home visits by social workers, Rob made it perfectly clear that if they did take him into care, he would run away and go back to his dad. It was decided that living with his father was probably best for him in the long term.

I have known Rob's dad since I was thirteen, when Rob and I first met. I spent a lot of time at their house as a teenager, and was accepted as part of Rob's circle of friends. However, the stronger my relationship became with Rob, the harder it was to hold on to a relationship with his dad. I think the final straw, in his eyes, was when many years later, Rob and I decided to buy a house together. He looked at this as me taking his son away which, added to my speaking well and having an opinion, I am sure makes him feel threatened by me, and no amount of effort on my part over the years has changed this. He has never liked his authority challenged, and in the past has openly undermined and disagreed with the way Rob and I have brought the boys up.

He is the way he is, and nothing will change that, but he has over many years drip-fed me snide remarks and said hurtful things, that make my relationship with him verge on the impossible. He changes the rules to suit himself, so it's 'be damned if you do, and be damned if you don't'. As parents, Rob and I instilled in the boys good manners – they cost nothing to give, but can make one's life run much more smoothly. When they were little and Rob's dad gave them sweets or a pound coin, and they said, 'thank you', the reply would be, 'You don't need to thank me for anything.' But woe-betide them if they forgot that 'thank you' – they would be branded 'rude and spoilt'.

Equally, praise is non-existent. When Zac was about three years old and first started nursery school, we encouraged him to go and tell his grandfather what he had learnt. So he said, 'Grandad, I can say my alphabet.' Rob's dad's only comment was, 'Yes, but can you say it backwards?' Zac, at twenty-one, still cannot say the alphabet backwards, but even if he could, he knows his grandfather's remark would probably be, 'Yes, but do you know the Chinese alphabet?'

The boys found his manner confusing and difficult to understand, and so over the years they stopped trying to engage him in conversation, or tell him about their lives. They struggled to have a good and meaningful relationship with him. It is a great pity, an opportunity lost.

However, Rob's sense of love and devotion goes deeper than simply something between father and son. He is fiercely loyal to his dad, no matter how frustrating his behaviour is, almost as though their roles have been reversed. He will not allow his dad's strange and difficult ways to tarnish what relationship they have, and many a time he has been the peace-maker. I am far less tolerant, and I simply cannot understand his father's dismissive and often damning behaviour, but it is one of the many attributes that I love about Rob – his devotion and sense of duty – even if I sometimes feel it is misplaced.

Grief is selfish, but our grief is more so than others' because he was our son and our pain is so much greater, darker, lonelier and all-consuming. Well, not really, but this is how it feels.

His dad cried, wished he had been in Lyneham, and said he felt he'd 'missed out.' 'No. Only when you have lost your son can you say you have missed out,' shouted Rob. His dad cried again – he doesn't really understand. He has never understood; he was not the same sort of parent as Rob. He will never understand the substance that binds us together or the glue that strangles us all at the same time. Maybe it's more like spider webs that are covered in glue. Sticky, invisible, always catching you when you least expect it, hiding in the corners ready to envelop us all.

We left after a couple of hours. There was nothing left to say, no more wondering what to talk about, no more wishing we were a million miles away. It needed to be done – duty and some sort of sense of love – but it was very hard. Rob's father and step-mother are old now, older than before. Looking at them, knowing they don't understand and never will should, I suppose, make me feel more sympathetic towards them – but it doesn't. They have their own grief, but some of that is borne of guilt. We are sorry for them, they so sorry for us – but sorry means nothing – so what is the point? There seems no time to stop and breathe – which is a good thing, as time lets you think. I don't want to think, it's all too new, too bleak and brutal.

Steely is playing drums in a band this evening. The band is being graded by their college tutors as part of their first year's final exams. He was racked with self-doubt. Would he be able to do this? Should he be doing this so soon – was it disrespectful? Would people judge him as uncaring? He knew he could never let anyone down, though, so he pushed through it. Rob, Zac and I went to watch and support him. I know what he is like – he stood tall he was doing this for Cyrus.

The 'grapevine' had been at work and the venue soon became awash with the boys' friends – young people drawn together to show their love and solidarity with Steely, and their pain at our loss. Rob moved through them during the evening, telling them that tonight we were here for Steely but that we would have a time for Cyrus the next day in our garden. 'Come about 1 pm and we will have a chance to talk then, and toast him properly,' he said.

Steely played; the band was good and I watched him with an overwhelming sense of love and pride. Oh God. Cyrus, I wish you could see your little brother.

My mother came down from Cambridge the next morning – Sunday; again someone who has guilt, but no glue. She brought a painting with her, wrapped in brown paper and string. It was one of an avocet that Cyrus would have inherited from her. Opening the door and seeing her standing there, I could feel myself shut down. The strain of our relationship over the past few years had finally taken its toll. I don't think it will ever recover; it's all too late and meaningless.

My mother, like Rob's dad, had little to do with the boys' lives. She was busy with a career and the social life she had built for herself in Cambridge. I know that parents differ in the ways they bring their children up, but sometimes it's the small things that are not done, that hurt so much.

When Zac was born, Rob and I were naturally thrilled; our first child a boy with fair hair, blue eyes. I assumed that she, as a grandparent, would be equally thrilled. He was six weeks old before she found the time to travel from Cambridge to Reading. I was so terribly hurt by her lack of interest, and perhaps that established the slippery slope we have now found our relationship on.

Yes, grief is selfish – but then so are people. Pain on pain is not helpful when dealing with glue – or am I just being spiteful because of this pain? No, many things have been done and not done, things that cannot be forgiven and now can never be repaired. That is another sadness I now bear.

She left just before the first of the boys' friends arrived. Zac, Sharpie and Steely had been to get food, plastic cups and bottles of Sambuca. As the afternoon wore on, more and more people arrived, our back garden littered with groups of young people, friends the boys have shared through their lives.

Ever since we moved to this house just ten days before Steely was born, our garden has been its focal point. The semi-detached 1950s house sits almost centrally in a 350-foot plot, set back on a narrow stretch of road, which is divided from the main road by a wide verge and trees. When we first moved in the garden was a bramble-filled wasteland. The house had been vacant for eighteen months, and the council had come in with its 'slash and burn' policy, leaving only a few plum trees, the odd rose and hundreds of nettles and brambles. Almost the first job Rob did was to build the boys a treehouse in a plum tree at the top of the garden. He planted some conifers to give the area a more secret feel. Sometimes, when the boys were a little older, and felt brave enough, they would spend the night in the treehouse, curled up in sleeping bags with Haribo sweets and plastic swords.

Slowly the garden took shape, flowerbeds were formed and planted with rhododendrons and bluebells, and ferns and lilies that were trampled accidentally and damaged by games of football. Cyrus and Steely were mad about the game, both involved in football teams as players and fans – Manchester United their club, like Rob. Zac would join in but he was always the one to kick the ball over the fences or break my shrubs. Even though he was never that interested in football, and still isn't, he would join in, never one to shirk out if there is a game and a laugh to be had.

Camouflage netting, woven into trees and across the top of the wooden bike-shed, provided cover for their army games. Ropes and pulleys were set from the loft windows to the bottom of the long front drive, and Action Men were dispatched, some with fire-crackers attached to them, the winner being the one whose man made it to the bottom or lost the fewest limbs, these often being the only time they really used the front garden to play in.

An above-ground swimming pool appeared one hot summer. It was more like vegetable soup than water with the number of children in it, but they loved it, shrieking with laughter as Rob's pot-holing wetsuits were used on those less sunny days. Cyrus was so skinny he looked like a piece of liquorice from a sherbet dib-dab. He was always the first to turn blue, even with the protection of the Neoprene suit, and needed a hot bath to de-frost. Extraordinary to think he joined the Army, training in some of the coldest places in the UK, and loved every minute of it.

After a couple of summers the games became too rough and the sides of the pool split, creating a huge wave that rushed down the back steps, subsiding just before it reached the back door, leaving a round barren patch where nothing would grow. The following year a trampoline took the pool's place, this too providing many hours of entertainment, children pinging off in different directions, with remarkably the only major casualty being the trampoline itself. Still, with thirteen kids all jumping on it at one time, it was hardly surprising it snapped shut on them like a Venus fly-trap. All this was a reflection of the childhood Rob wished he himself could have had – nothing brought him more pleasure than seeing the boys and their friends having fun.

As the boys' needs changed, Rob gave up his garage, deciding that building materials were better stored at the builder's merchants. He put up a stud wall, creating a separate toilet; carpet tiles went down on the concrete floor, and a television, an old stereo and sofa were installed. The boys and their friends now had a warm, dry place to meet. The breeze-block walls were painted white, and over the years have become covered in graffiti, photo-collages, song lyrics, poems and drawings, all of their friends contributing to the décor. When Steely got his first drum kit, it too found a home there. The garage gave them somewhere to be, other than on street corners or down by the river.

By the time Zac was fourteen he was smoking cigarettes, and our attitude was; better we know and he smokes here, rather than sneaking off and doing it behind our backs. Cyrus soon joined him, both in the smoking and being in the garage. He had tried hanging around on street corners but got cold and wet, and eventually decided he was better off in the comfort of the garage.

The boys bought themselves Play Stations and games with money they'd saved from doing morning paper-rounds – something they all started at the age of twelve, getting up early no matter what the weather because, as Rob said, 'You will never have an easier job than pushing papers through peoples' letter-boxes.' Hours of Pro-football, fantasy adventures and racing games were played in the garage. Some nights there were over twenty of them in there, music blaring, shouting, singing and laughing. Fortunately, we have understanding and forgiving neighbours. Their friends became part of our family.

I can only remember one fight, and that was between two of their friends when too much beer had been consumed. The boys didn't really fight when they were children – they often argued, but there was rarely blood drawn. Cyrus would always have to have the last word, which frequently got him into trouble with Rob and me, and I'm sure that Steely, as the youngest, was pushed about and dominated by him – so that he was completely clear as to his place in the pecking order. Steely adored him – and no-one else was allowed to push his little brother around; he was fiercely protective of him and would have come down very hard on anyone who tried.

So, that Sunday afternoon once again all were welcomed. We needed them; they needed us. They sat quietly talking, crying, reminiscing. Wandering through them I was touched by the stories I overheard – stories of Cyrus, and how he had always managed to find time for each of them when home on leave, stories of antics at school, long evenings spent here in our converted garage, impromptu 'gatherings' in the garden – so many good times. The boys are well loved by their friends, and Rob and I are always included, treated with respect and friendship by them all – I know how much they will all miss him.

We already know we won't have a wake, now is the time to celebrate his life – while we have the energy and his friends have the need. So Cyrus's iPod was put on shuffle and his eclectic taste in music filled the air – many smiled at memories the music evoked. Then a song I was vaguely familiar with, brought a complete hush from those within earshot. Rob was sitting on a low wall by one of the ponds, and only the sound of the waterfall interrupted. It was 'If I could turn back the hands of time' by R. Kelly – unbelievable – and the song took everyone's breath away, making every track after seem somehow insignificant.

A toast with Sambuca, four bottles gone in an instant – over 75 plastic shot glasses, filled with the drink Cyrus loved, shared with Zac and Rob every time he was home – it too will always hold memories; I don't think any of us can drink it without him cascading into our minds.

At 10 pm, exhausted, we pushed the last of them out of the gate and down the driveway. Clearing up Rob put the iPod on again, asking Zac to find the R. Kelly track. Over and over, long after the leftover food was thrown away and the bottles and tins put into plastic bags, the track repeated itself. It was that evening we decided this piece of music would be played at his funeral.

I don't want to look at flowers or cards any more, but they keep arriving. I know that people mean well, but they don't understand. I don't understand, so I don't know why I think they should. Lilies used to remind me of birth – Zac's birth, and those happy days when the world was rosy and I was naïve. Now they remind me of death and yet I love them still – am I mad?

Hours turn into days, but I'm not sure when these start or finish. Nothing is clear any more – days, hours, minutes all merge in and out of each other. Flowers and cards – I don't want any more fucking flowers.

How do I deal with the anger of a seventeen-year-old and the loneliness of a twenty-one-year old? I know that we all have to travel along this path at our own speeds, but trying to explain and come to terms with it is exhausting. At seventeen, Steely wants to move on and away from the pain, Zac wants to stay but needs the pain to go – or at least know when it will go. That is an answer I just don't have. I don't know the best way to deal with this grief. I cannot be angry because I don't know who to be angry with, but I understand the frustration that Steely feels. He needs to move on and feels that by showing he is sad makes it take longer – and is not what Cyrus would have wanted.

I know what Cyrus would have wanted, but he can't have it yet. It is all still too soon, festering in our minds and hearts. He would have hated the thought of our pain and the fact that he is the cause of it, and yet that's not what he ever thought would happen. He didn't go out there to die. He went out there to fulfil his dream and come home. He did fulfil his dream, but unfortunately he left us here wishing his dream hadn't had to come at such a price.

He has gone and left us behind, trying to make sense of what has happened – trying to come to terms with the impossible. He has left a huge, gaping hole that will never be filled and I don't think any of us really want it to be filled – just not there in the first place.

I will always have three sons. I just wish it hadn't been that one was only borrowed for such a short time. I need my three sons and my man. I don't think I had ever really needed anything before this – not true need in this sense. This has fused Rob and I together, our souls interwoven with love for each other and a pain shared. I want to go back, to start again but to have a different ending. But then I suppose to start again would still lead to this place, because I wouldn't change a second of any of the things that went before. To do that would be to change us and I don't want to do that. I just want a different ending.

Letters came too, not just cards. Some meant more than others.

> *Dear Rob and Helena,*
>
> *My name is Paul Mervis and I was Cyrus's Platoon Commander in 2 Rifles. I was very close with Cyrus and he asked me before we left that if anything were to happen to him that he would like me to speak to you. Unfortunately I am not back until the beginning of July and our grief must remain with us here. I just wanted to write to you to express mine and the Platoon's deep sorrow at the passing of your much beloved son.*
>
> *Right now, I feel like a part of me has been removed. I know that some of the men are absolutely devastated. If this is how we feel I can only begin to appreciate the pain that you must*

be going through. Cyrus was such a special boy. I remember the first interview that I had with him when he joined the Battalion. He was so shy but spoke to me with a maturity far greater than all the other young men that would sit at the other side of my desk. I still have it written in my notes – he just wanted to be a good Rifleman, not the RSM or join the SAS. Little did I know what a huge part of our lives he would become.

The first time I really got to know Thatch was on the exercise in Salisbury Plain where he won the valour award and was sent skydiving. That was the first time I learned about all his fears, which remarkably included the robin redbreast, perhaps one of the most inoffensive of birds. When he told me about his fear of flying, I could think of no one better to be thrown out of a plane. In reality, whatever phased Thatch, he would overcome with an understated courage. It was seen when he sky dived but I saw it every day in Afghanistan, I could have asked him to do anything. He was a brave, courageous man.

Thatch used to frustrate me because he was so intelligent. Whenever someone comes across my desk who has the potential to take his academic abilities further I always try to persuade them to get qualifications through the army. Thatch would stand before you sparkling with natural intellect, in the way he analysed events or simply just in the way he talked and the way no one could win a ripping session with him. He just told me flat out that if he wanted to continue his education he would have stayed at school. That was that. No matter how hard I tried, when Thatch was determined there was nothing you could do.

He was mature far beyond his years – something that I can only attribute to you. He would talk about Rob with a reverence and respect that was perhaps a little unusual in a Rifleman. He loved his family completely. I remember once, catching a plane from Belfast back to London. I was walking down the aisle and I saw Thatch with his cheeky smile patting the seat next to him. I sat and spoke with Thatch for over an hour about ISAs and PEPs, savings and capital, discussed the housing market and what we both wanted by the end of our twenties. I walked away wiser, having spoken to an eighteen year old with more sensible advice than me. That and all Cyrus's wonderful attributes are a credit to you.

It would be impossible to remember or recount every joke I had with Cyrus or every fond memory, but a summer I will now never forget was in Kosovo last year when we were stuck 'defending' a forsaken monastery in the middle of nowhere. I bought a chess set and was desperate to play with someone. Who would step up but Cyrus who would play me at chess from morning until night? Improving all the time, I am sure there was a glint of triumphalism when he won his first game off me. I wasn't surprised. I would talk to him for hours over those chess games, mostly about inconsequential things, but Cyrus could balance meaningful conversation with jokes easily.

The other side of Thatch, behind all the jokes and laughter, that I flatter myself I perhaps saw more than anyone else in the army, was his caring and thoughtful side. Thatch would always find time to confide in me and I would look forward to the time when I could sit down with him. He would screw up his face slightly into his thoughtful, serious look and we would discuss his future plans, his love life, other people in the Platoon, the fate of the Afghan people. Behind all the jokes Thatch would always be sensitive to how others were feeling and doing. I would always have to stop myself confiding too much in him, trying to keep the line between Officer and Rifleman, now I wish we could have spoken more.

During PDT training Thatch was a reliable as ever. It has already been mentioned in the eulogy but he was so competent that he could as a Rifleman, take a Section and lead it in a demanding attack completely unphased. He was central to the Platoon.

My next and last memory of Thatch, the one that I will cherish for the rest of my life was one evening in the FOB. I was the night watch keeper, which essentially meant that I had to stay up all night in case anything untoward happened. Joe Ells, who like me knew Thatch from the beginning and had always been Thatch's Section Commander, was the Guard Commander. We were sitting in the Operations Room bored, when we heard Thatch's and Pricey's voices on the radio from Sangar 1. We told them to make us brews and they told us to get lost. The usual banter! Joe and I decided that we would go down there and give him a dig, he used to bring out all our inner children. We caught him on his way back to bed. He stopped, gave us that same cheeky smile and sprinted away laughing. I chased him, there wasn't a hope in hell of me catching him though. We were in the green zone, in a tiny outpost, the IED belt was in, casualties were being taken across the battle group, the Taliban were closing in but that night, that part of Afghanistan, the FOB echoed to the sound of his laughter. I will cherish that memory until the day I die.

When I spoke to the Platoon after his death, I told them that I loved him like a son. It was the only way I could articulate my grief. On reflection I realise, that I hardly knew him, and if he could have that effect on me in two short years that I can only imagine the sense of loss that you

feel. The only words of solace that I can offer are that when he died, he died surrounded by people who loved him.

As soon as I return to the UK, I would like to come and speak to you. I will understand if you may not want this and will respect your wishes whatever they may be. If there is anything you want to know in the near future I will leave my e-mail address and you can get in touch with me through that.

All my sympathy
Paul Mervis, OC 10 Platoon, C Company

Despite all the horror and anguish of the past few days, here was a letter from the front line, from someone who knew Cyrus, had known him over the past two years. Our connection with him, hope within this agony of loss. Yes, of course we wanted to meet Paul, talk to him, listen to the stories, and grasp one more chance to live the life of our son through his recollections. Here in this gloom was a shining light. Strange to think that someone we'd not met could suddenly mean so much. We so needed to meet him. I emailed him that afternoon: 'Yes, please come and see us as soon as you are able.'

The fact that they all miss him so much hurts too. As Paul said, they only knew each other for two years and yet, in the way they live their soldier's lives, they become one big family – laughing, crying, bleeding and dying for each other. They take it all in their stride – but hurt so very deeply, just as we do. My heart burns for all of them – these losses they have, these sacrifices they make, these men for whom my heart bleeds every time I hear those dreadful words, 'The family have been informed'. They too are family; they too have altered lives now.

Ian phoned the next day. He had good news and bad; would we be in later so he could come to see us. What possible good news could he have? A mistake and they had got it wrong? Cyrus wasn't dead – it was a case of mistaken identity? In my heart I knew this wasn't the news we were going to hear.

We sat down with Ian, always so professional, so kind in this time of dreadful minutes and hours. So, to the good news – we needed some. Ian had been contacted by the Coroner's Office and they had said that we would be able to see Cyrus one last time. Good news? To be able to see my dead son one more time? Yes – fantastically it was the best news we'd heard since that horrific opening of the door to the faces of those two men and their words of death which left a family ruined. How cruel good news can be.

But then, to the bad. Surely there cannot be any worse than we've already been told. But there's no card too savage to be dealt. What a kick in the stomach. Lieutenant Paul Mervis (Mad Dog) had died in a blast in Afghanistan just that morning, ten days after Cyrus.

Of all the letters we received, dead men wrote the ones that I will treasure, the ones that mean the most to me. Other letters are written by people you know you will never meet or want to see – royals, government officials, army personnel, long-lost friends and Sir Alex Ferguson. Oh, how Cyrus would have loved to see that letter. How ironic that we got Paul's letter the day before he was killed, so he wouldn't have read our email. How monstrous – glue returns. Letters from families who have the same pain as we do – the same sticky substance in their veins. All of us now have a common agony. I want to give mine away – but who the hell would want it? More to the point, who the hell would I give it to? No one deserves this; no parent should have to bury their child.

I have a new skin. It doesn't fit and gives me blisters. I wonder how long it will take for the skin to harden and get used to the new pressure points. Some places will always have to be bandaged and bathed. I don't think they will ever harden and accept that new skin.

Sometimes, when I wake in the night, I think that I've got my old skin back – but then I feel the blisters start to burn. Conscious thought is cruel. My mind wanders away from the awful and zigzags along, making new thoughts. When I get to the end I always ask myself how I got there in the first place, and then all the zigzags unfurl and take me screaming back to the awful. I can't stop that zigzag process. Why does it have to go back to the beginning? Why can't it just stay in that slightly confused state, and not question the road it took to get there? My mind is torturing me and there seems no relief.

Perhaps the glue is depression. I hate that word. My mother is a psychiatrist and it makes me remember visiting old men in filthy pyjamas with their bottoms hanging out, in long, cold wards at 'The Hospital'. That was Borocourt Hospital, Rotherfield Peppard, Oxfordshire, that had originally been built as Wyfold Manor House in 1878, and had been purchased by Berkshire, Buckinghamshire and Oxfordshire County Councils in 1930 as an institute for 'mental defectives'. It was closed in 1993 and sold when patients and staff moved into smaller units throughout the counties. The main building was converted into private flats in 2000. This was where my mother worked, helping those poor souls who had lost their way – and sometimes we would go with her. Now I know how they feel – but I still never want to visit those corridors again. We were so frightened of those men with their grey whiskers and even greyer faces. Dead eyes – they all had dead, unseeing eyes. I don't think mine are dead yet – just unseeing, shrouded in glue and pain. No, I don't want to go there again – it was a cold and scary place.

I'm not scared – but I do feel cold. People we've met along this journey say we are 'fantastic and amazing'.

I certainly don't feel either of those things. How I am is just how I have to be. I guess Cyrus's strength of character came from somewhere, but I don't feel strong – just sad... so very, very sad. I'm not the sort of person to sit and wail in a corner and tear my hair out, but I'm not strong. Perhaps 'determined' is a better word to use. I'm determined to make sure that the pride I feel for my children is shared with others, and that it doesn't get lost in the grief. They carry themselves so well, my men, and I need to make sure that they don't have to carry me too. I must use my own strength to move forward, not rely on theirs – that would be too crippling for them and I have never wanted to be a burden.

Have you ever been to the seaside and stood barefoot on the edge of the sea? The waves move in and out – no way of stopping them. Even if you dig your heels into the sand as hard as you can, when the tide recedes it trickles out from underneath them. My pain is like that. I can't stop it, no matter how hard I tread in the sand.

CHAPTER 4

A B WALKER & SONS

Coroners, DNA testing and Orders of Service. Why would I want to know anything about them? Where do we begin? Serjeant Major Lee Jones would help us (the spelling of Sergeant with a 'j' is unique to The Rifles). Body parts. Blast victim. Not sure what condition he is in. What the hell does that mean? Can we see him? Do I want to? No. Yes. He is one of my babies – of course I want to see him – but not in a coffin with white silk strategically positioned around him.

The glue is now in my lungs, choking me – trying to drown me. What happened to my life? How do I do this? Where are the markers? Where is the page to turn that helps me through and guides me along? There are no markers or pages… I have to make this up as I go. I don't want to do this, but I can't stop it.

Men visiting, talking about precision marching, coffin-bearing, Order of Service, cars and coffins. I don't understand what is happening here. My family was not supposed to have to choose hymns or tell their friends that their brother and son had died. Someone is going to tell me that it isn't real and he will be ringing any minute now, asking us to collect him from the airport. No – now it's just glue and the flowers that need sorting because the water is starting to smell and they make me feel sick.

The Reverend Canon Brian Shenton came to our house because he would be leading the funeral service. Sitting at the dining room table, he explained the basic order of the service and asked if we had any particular items we would like included. He also shared his sorrow at our loss. We are not religious people and had not realised the significance of Saint Mary the Virgin Church, which is a Minster. 'Minster' is a title given to large or important churches, and Reading Minster is a Grade I listed building, extensively restored from 1551 to 1555 with stone and timber from the ruins of Reading Abbey, where Henry I is buried. Ian Tindall, our Visiting Officer, had suggested the Minster for its status, central location in Reading and capacity to accommodate a full military funeral. It was beginning to dawn on us that this until-now surreal situation was becoming reality. This very beautiful church that we'd walked past countless times on our way into town is, coincidentally, less than a hundred metres from the Army Recruitment Office where Cyrus made his pledge to Queen and Country just two and a half years before. Now this church was going to become the focal point of his funeral. It's all incomprehensible.

The Canon continued and explained that there would be an opportunity to have a piece of music of our choice during the entry. The Sentences, followed by the Introduction, Prayers of Penitence, the Regimental Collect, the Lesson, a hymn, the Eulogies read on behalf of Lieutenant Colonel Rob Thomson, Commanding Officer, 2nd Battalion, The Rifles and a letter read on behalf of Serjeant Leon Smith, Cyrus's Platoon Serjeant. This would be followed by the Address, which would be given by the Dean – then the final hymn followed by, at our request, the Lord's Prayer, Commendation, the Blessing, and then another piece of music to exit.

He asked us what hymns we would like, and I was at a loss. Suddenly all hymns I knew disappeared from my mind. Rob said he would like 'Abide With Me' as he had always liked it, and it was one he thought most people would recognise. We knew there would be a large number of young people attending, and wanted this service to mean something to them too. A hymn recognised, even if only by the music, is still one they were more likely to sing. A second hymn seemed harder to choose somehow – we were unsure, then the Canon suggested 'Lord of All Hopefulness', which is apparently used frequently in Army services. He thought that once we heard it, we would recognise it. Before he left, he said he would leave the choice of the entrance and exit music to us, and that A B Walker & Sons would coordinate with him before the day.

After he had gone, we got out the laptop and listened to 'Lord of All Hopefulness', which in fact we had both heard before. It seemed the Canon's suggestion was more than appropriate, so this was to be the second hymn. It was hard to find a balance, being non-religious, choosing pieces of music, hymns and prayers that merge easily and transcend all beliefs without offending, while being acutely aware of the honour bestowed upon us by being able to use the wonderful Minster. The Canon was incredibly gracious and simply stated that it was our day, to honour our son, and he would do everything in his power to make it as smooth and painless a process as possible.

I've never been in a funeral director's offices before. We sat in the car and tried to compose ourselves before we went in. This is just not right, my legs won't work, and my mouth is dry. I just want to run away and pretend it's not happening – but I guess they recognise the look of the lost. The young receptionist said how sorry she was, that she had been at school with Cyrus and on her first day he'd shared a cigarette behind the bike shed with her. This can't be – it's not true, not my son, not here in a room in a box.

We were shown into an office and introduced to Carolyn, who would be looking after us, and who had been taking care of Cyrus since he arrived from the Radcliffe Hospital in Oxford. I remember noticing the paintings in the office and reception area, and thinking how unusual they were; black, orange and red naked men with their arms spread – going upwards to heaven, if that's what you believe. Moving out of this life, and away from those that love them.

Carolyn helped us fill in forms – what we would like put into the paper, how we wanted the booklets to look that would be placed on the pews in the Minster. I've no idea what went into the paper and I've never looked at the booklet since. We talked about the music that would be played for the entrance and exit. We wanted 'If I could turn back the hands of time', played as we followed the Bearer Party carrying Cyrus into the Minster, then 'Ave Maria' at the end of the service as we left. We were unsure as to whether or not our first choice was appropriate in such a church. Carolyn smiled and said, 'It's your day – you can choose which ever music means the most to you, and we'll make sure the Canon receives a CD with the pieces on before the Service.' Everything was overwhelming.

It was then time to go and spend one last moment with him. Just the five of us in a room, our whole family together, for one last time. 'I don't know if I can do this,' I whispered to Rob. He just looked at me and said, 'Well, you can either come in or wait in the car, it's up to you.' I needed him to say that, to snap me out of my moment of panic and self-pity. No choice – no question about what I was going to do. I just needed him to help me stand. I should have been helping him – we needed to help each other and the boys. I felt weak and useless. I couldn't do any of this without Rob.

The door opened and there he was, all alone, lying there dead. He looked so little in the coffin – pale and cold. His dark strawberry-blonde almost-red hair, was longer than I imagined it would be. He was so proud of his looks with his pale freckled skin, arching eyebrows and slim straight nose. Now his lips were thin and tinged with blue, he had slight grazes on his chin and forehead that had been masked to try and soften their severity. He looked so little. I remember him being so much taller than me – so lithe and athletic, so handsome. My handsome men... and now one was dead. This was just too much for one heart to bear. I was too short to kiss him, but I stroked his hair and face – his cold, hard face. He was always so full of life, always smiling. He had such corn-flower blue eyes, framed by long, fair eyelashes, and now they were closed and I couldn't see their colour.

He still had the cigarette that Zac had rolled for him in Lyneham, together with the yellow clipper lighter. Such a small thing, but the effect it had on us was huge – how kind everyone was who had been involved in his final journey, to make sure that these items were still with him – a mark of respect, both for him and us. We took a bottle of Sambuca and a shot glass; the boys and Rob had one last drink with him. I couldn't. We left the partially drunk bottle and glass in the coffin against his arm. Zac rolled him another cigarette and placed it in his breast pocket.

Captain Richard Sellars had asked us how we wanted him dressed. 'Combats', we'd said. He died in combat – he should be buried in combats. He would have looked so wrong in his dress uniform. He looked so wrong anyway – so still, so empty. Where was my boy? Where had his essence gone?

I left the room first. Someone had to make the first move and I didn't think I could bear to see him like that any more. Steely was going to be the last one to leave – he had his own last message – words only for Cyrus, and he had things he wanted to leave in with him. I don't know what – only he and Cyrus will know. All those nights they shared, talking to each other through their bedroom wall; all those years they shared. They needed one more secret. He so loved his older brother. Oh God, Steely, how the hell do we move forward from this?

As we took our last look, Rob asked, 'All right mate?' Steely's nod was barely noticeable. 'Yeah,' was the whispered reply – and we walked away and closed the door. Steely hadn't planned to leave it, and I'm not sure he was aware he had, but he left his childhood in that room that day. I hoped he wouldn't be too long inside – I needed to go. I couldn't be here any longer. We sat in the car numb, almost unable to leave, knowing there would now be only the four of us. Would I ever get used to that number? No.

I live in pockets of time. They have no seconds, minutes or hours. They are just pockets. Some are deeper than others. Some are clear, but most are dark and scary. I don't like being alone in those pockets, but like my nightmares they are mine, and I can't share them. They are my own personal sores. Sores that weep, and no matter how much you clean them, they don't scab over and heel... like my blistering skin.

I want my 'normal' back – my 'ordinary'. There is no anger, just pain – hot searing pain, that electrocutes you, causing blisters and opening those festering sores. I put on my brave face, but I have to strangle the screams in case they jump out and bite the faces off the people around me.

When I'm alone I'm not so brave. The sobs come in waves, racking my body and leaving me exhausted. Sometimes I have to stuff my fingers into my mouth to stop myself from sobbing.

I'm now part of an exclusive group that I've no wish to be in. Every death is personal, but now I share a common agony. Stripped entirely of any power to do anything to help, I feel useless. What do I say to someone else who is going through this? How can I be of use? Perhaps just knowing how they feel is enough; they too will understand in time, I guess, as more and more of us join this group.

As a mother I'm supposed to be able to make things better for my children – bathe their grazes and soothe their fevers. I can't help Zac and Steely though. I can't kiss it better and make the pain go away; this is another torture I face. How can it be that this has happened and I have no way of making it better? It rips me apart knowing that Rob and the boys are suffering, and there is nothing I can do to help. I feel useless. All my instincts are to nurture and protect – but this is out of my league, and I'm at a loss as to what to do. I can't even help myself, so I know rationally there is nothing I can do to help them – but you can't stop instincts.

It's the loss of power and one's ability to help, knowing Rob as I do – someone who has always been able to make everything ok, fiercely devoted to us as a family, strong and capable, hard-working and honest – reduced to a shell. I am completely unable to help this man whom I have loved since we first met at school in Henley-on-Thames when I was thirteen and he fourteen. His fair hair now shows signs of greying over his ears, and his eyes have lost their deep blue lustre. We've lost our youth. We've lost ourselves. The people we were have gone.

What does our future hold? Everything we do goes back to the fact that we have three sons – but now only two remain. It throws us off balance. I used to struggle with three small children because I had only two hands to hold them. Now I long for that struggle again. With every new child I grew a new heart – a heart that was as full and capable of loving as my others, a heart for each child. I have a lifeless heart now, still full of love but empty all the same... a space that cannot flourish any more. My other hearts will continue to grow, and with each new second of my children's lives they will swell and make room... but one remains the same size, never to bloom again. It hurts because it can't grow, but it will never go or fade – just sit there in my chest as a constant reminder that I have three children.

If sorrow were an old coat it would be nice to be able to take it off for a day, and be relieved of the weight of it. I know that I would have to put it back on again, but it would be an attractive thought, to be able to unburden myself for a while. I need a means whereby I can extract the agony from my brain. Sometimes I think I'm going to implode from the sheer pressure.

Arriving home, exhausted with the whole process, I thought I'd already plummeted the lowest level I could possibly reach – but that was deeper than low. Nothing can be as wretched as the things we have just had to do. Say 'goodbye', take one last look, one last touch, one last secret. This is the ultimate pain, and the last time we would ever see him.

We just sat, unable to talk, too wrapped up in our own glue to help each other. Nothing could be said to erase those awful memories – nothing can be said to make it better. My splintered family – my men gone in a moment, never to be the same again. Changed.

It wasn't in the kitchen – nowhere near it, in fact – and Steely was the one who found it, in a small white-painted wooden box that had been my younger brother Sam's toy-box, and which Cyrus had used as a bedside table. The 'Sam' box was the keeper of this treasure. A couple of hours after we had come back from saying our last goodbyes to our most precious soldier-son, Steely was going through some of Cyrus's things and he came across it.

'I've found it! He did write a letter,' Steely said, coming downstairs two at a time. He held it as though it was an ice-cube that might melt in his hands, and then sat down with us and read it out loud. He was so brave reading it, tears streaming down his cheeks, sobbing uncontrollably and choking on the words, absolutely determined to carry on, no matter how much they burned and twisted into his heart and brain.

CHAPTER 5

THE LAST LETTER

He had written something to each of us. How he managed to write such a letter I'll never know. Magnificent, amazing, brave, kind and thoughtful are just some of the words that spring to mind when I think of him in his room, writing to us before he had even left the country. How the hell do you write a letter to be opened on your death? I don't think I could do it and I'm so proud of him for having done it. What a man. I so wish we had never had to see its contents; I wish he had been able to retrieve it and take it away with him. I wish he had never had to write it. I just wish he was here.

In his letter his intention was to leave us the tools to carry on. He simply didn't think that it would take us a lifetime to learn to use them – if we manage to learn at all. I miss him so much. I can't take in the fact that I'll never see him again. It doesn't make sense to me somehow. It shouldn't be happening to us. It doesn't seem real.

①

hello its me, this is gunna be hard for you to Read but I wrote this knowing everytime you thinks shits got to much for you to handle (so dont cry on it MUM!!) you can Read this and hopefully it will help you all get through.

For a start SHIT I got hit!! now Iv got that out the way I can say the things Iv hopefully made clear, or if I havent this should clear it all up for me. My hole life you'v all been there for me through thick and thin bit like a wedding through good and bad without you I believe I wouldnt have made as far as I have. I Died doing what I was born to do I was happy and felt great about myself although the Army was sadly The ending of me @ it was also the making of me so please dont feel any hate toward it. One thing I no I never made clear to you all was I make jokes about my life starting In the Army

→

That's wrong. VERY wrong my life began a LONG time befor That (OBVIOUSLY) but you get what I mean. All the times Iv tried to neglect The family, get angry when you try teach me wrong from Right (The other way round) wot I mean to say is I only realised That you were trying to help when I joined The army and without YOUR help I would have never of had The BALLS the GRIT and the dam right Determanation to crack on and do it. If I could have a wish In life it would of to be able to say Iv gone and done things Many would never try to do, And going to Ayghan has forfilled my dream ie my goal. Yes I am young wich as a parent must brake you heart, but you must all Somehow find The strength that I found to do Something no matter how big The challenge. As Im writing This letter I can see you all Crying and mornin my death but If I could have one wish In an "After life" it would be to Stop your Crying and continueing your dreams. (as I did)

③

because if I were watching only That would brake my heart. So dry your tears and put on a brave face for the rest of you friends and family who need you with my death will come money! NO!! - Thats The last Thing Anyone wants to be thinking of but when you have put on your brave faces and find That strength to go on. I want each and everyone of you to fulfill a dream and at The end of it look at what you have done (completed) and feel The accomplishment and achievment I did only then will you understand how I felt when I passed away. Zac, I want you to buy this bloody house and do it up I mean really do it up take time and pride in it love it be Interested In it because you are a very special person you are kind you have a true heart and That you will find 1 in a million. This will carry you Through life. Steely, Steely Steely Steely where do I start with you, you of all The family I look up to

66

④

The mask, no drugs, no smoking, no
bullying, you are just a happy bloke
and That made me jealous, not in a
Friday the 13th way, where I'd
wanna hurt you for it but That also
is extremly hard to find. True happyness.
you are both amazing men and will
continue to be throughout your
lives you both deserve to be happy
and fulfill all of your dreams.
Dad - my idol, my friend, my best friend
my teacher, my coach, everything I
ever succeeded in my life I owe to
you and maybe a little bit of me!
you are a great man and the perfect
role model and The past 16 years of
being in The Army I noticed That, and
me and you's have been on The best
level we have ever been. I Thank you
for nothing because I no all you have
given to me is not there to be Thanked
for its There because you did it cause
you love me and That is my most
prouddest Things I could ever Say.

Mum, where do i start with you!!. for a start your perfect. forget the touching me at times i didnt wanna be touche i.e football, you really were perfect your smell your hugs the way your life was dedicated to us boy and especially the way you cared each and every step us boys took. i Love you, you were the reason i made it as far as i did. you were the reason i was loved more than any child i no and that made me feel special. Your all such great Individuals and i hope some how this letter will help you get through this shit time!! just remember do NOT mourn my death as hard as this will seem, celebrate a great life that has had its ups and downs i love you all more than you would ever no and in your own Individual ways helped me get through it all. i wish you all the best with your dreams. Remember chin up head down with love cyrus xxxx

I'm not sure how much pain one heart can take, and I really do understand now how people die of broken hearts. I'm not going to die just yet, but sometimes it feels like it. It would be a relief from this desolateness I feel on a daily basis – but I could never leave Rob, Zac and Steely. I've not even considered taking my own life – that would seem such a selfish way out. Yet I'm not sure if you have reached that stage in the agony that is your life, that you are actually thinking straight about the consequences, and the people you leave behind. It is the people who have to carry on that the pain never leaves.

I know that I will always have this pain. Like the glue, it's now part of my soul and nothing but my own death will alleviate it – this selfish glue that has settled in my veins. My death will come when it's ready but not now, and I'll not have a hand in speeding it up.

Perhaps we are born with a time-line. None of us knows the length of that line and so, if we are lucky and determined enough, we live our lives as if every day was our last, enabling us to squeeze in everything we can before the end of the line is reached. If this is so, then I would like to think that Cyrus did just that. He did everything he wanted to do before his time was up – or at least as much as he could manage in nineteen and a half years. I think he did, and this is partly what he was trying to tell us in his letter. I know he knew how very much we loved him.

They are all so different, my boys – such different personalities, likes and dislikes. Steely obsessed with drumming and a desire for life, with a drive that will ultimately see him make a career in music – and a sense of humour that will ensure he will never be without a circle of good friends.

Zac hasn't found his niche. Another music lover, going to as many festivals and concerts as he can throughout the year, a head-banger with his fair hair and goatie beard. He works with Rob at the moment, he's good with his hands, is artistic and has a heart of gold. He will do well in life, has the right attitude – is made of the right stuff.

Then there was Cyrus, who wanted to join the Army. The middle son, the obsessive one who constantly craved attention as a child. He too loved music; Motown, Michael Jackson, Eminem, rap and hip-hop – and even the occasional heavy metal track. A perfectionist when it came to his looks – hair had to be 'just so'; his clothes – designer labels and snug-fitting, so as to show off his muscles; being a soldier, had to be the best at everything; competitive, aggressive, noisy, fun and loyal. He was the 137th serviceman to die from hostile fire in Afghanistan, while the deaths from enemy action in Iraq stand at 136. He would have liked that – being the one that tipped the scales. It would have made him feel important. He was important, is important, will forever be important.

Sometimes they shared a look, a tilt of the head, the way the corners of their mouths twitched when they teased each other. A confident gait, blue eyes, two red-heads and one fair – not 'peas in a pod' as so many other families are. I hope Zac and Steely manage to fulfil their dreams and live the best lives they can, even though they have been touched by tragedy. Perhaps it will make them stronger people – kinder and more understanding of others and their weaknesses. Well, I suppose it will or it won't, but that is something that I can have no hand in. They have to lead their own lives, and make their own decisions. I will be there to help and support if they need me, but they are men now, and I have to stand back and watch.

I know they will always make me proud. They are the sort of people that others like to be around. I like being around them – they make me smile. I love them and I hope they will always know that I do.

Cyrus's letters from the front line and his last letter were published in The Independent because of a chance meeting with the journalist Terri Judd in Wootton Bassett. She had asked us if we had received any letters whilst he was in Afghanistan, and if so could she see them, as she was writing a piece about soldiers' letters home. We agreed and she came to see us a couple of days later. She read the seven that he'd written and then asked if he'd left a last letter. We weren't quite sure what to say – it was such a personal letter. These were his final words to us as a family, and we had been the only ones to read them. She explained that she had written one to her mother as she had been out to both Iraq and Afghanistan, and after talking to some other soldiers, realised that it was something quite a few of them did, so it made sense to write one of her own – just in case. Rob and I were reluctant at first; Zac was away and Steely not too keen. He thought that it was addressed to us and it should remain that way, but we agreed that she could read it and see what she thought. 'It's amazing. If you could share this with people it would be fantastic, as he has said things many people only think and don't dare write down,' was what she said. We decided to let

71

her take a copy, and we agreed that there were certain parts (to the boys) that we would omit because, as Steely said, they were personal to them and he didn't want it all public.

What a response. Who would have thought that those letters could have had such an impact on people? Both radio and television interviews came on the back of their publication. It was his last one that really struck people. Grown men were having to pull over into lay-bys because they were crying. Oh God, Cyrus, if only you knew. Such wise words from someone so young. You have touched so many lives, my darling. I wish you knew.

How can it be that I'll never see him again? The searing pain keeps getting stronger, eating into the fibres of my body, corroding me from inside. I can feel it well up from my toes. It makes my bones ache. This sadness is overwhelming – it consumes me, stopping me in my tracks and paralysing me. I seem constantly to be searching for soggy tissues tucked into waistbands or pockets of jeans.

I'm sure I'm depressed. I've talked about that before, but I think I am. I don't want to go to the doctor, though. They have enough to deal with because of all this swine flu stuff. Anyway, I don't think a pill can help mend a broken heart. There are no words of comfort, and no magic cure. This will just have to run its course and drag me with it.

I see his face, those blue, blue eyes. That smile. The trouble is you can't hear a smile or see those eyes blink again. How the hell do I go on? Where am I going on to? What do I do when I get there – if I get there? I don't want this to be happening. I want him back home. Not under a mound of dirt that we tend like a treasured garden. Just home, safe and alive. But I know I can't have that wish – not now, not ever. It's more than I can bear at times. Now is one of those times. I'm not having a very good morning so far. Perhaps this afternoon will be better.

You can't properly describe dreams or nightmares, and I think it is the same with grief. In your head it makes sense, but when you say the words out loud to someone else, they become jumbled and confused. They then confuse me, and I get to the point when I'm not really sure they made sense in the first place, even though they were straight in my head to begin with. Perhaps this truly is madness. Yes – I think I'm mad. There. I've said it now.

It doesn't make me feel better though, admitting I'm mad. It's that glue again, clogging my thoughts, making everything confused and sticky. Enough now, I'll write again but enough for today.

I wonder if someone else will read this one-day and understand. I hope so. I hope that this strange collection of words will bring comfort to someone somewhere. I know I'm not the only person in the world who feels like this. I am very lonely, though. Grief *is* lonely. It's like lying on your back in the dark, being swept along a cold underwater river. Freezing water seeps into your very being, disabling you, making it impossible to determine up from down or left from right. Or perhaps it's a cold fog, moving across the river. Everything is disjointed and moves at a different pace. I feel like I'm looking down at myself, but if I reach out I can't touch anything. Perhaps this is an out-of-body experience.

When I first looked at the photos that we had developed from his camera, it was like looking at someone else's life. Now when I look at them I know that they *are* of him and his life in Afghanistan and before, and I find them so much harder to look at. One of Cyrus and Paul Mervis, standing between two Military Police Officers on a dirt road in Kosovo. Still in Kosovo, Cyrus with a radio head-set on, sitting in front of a wall studded with bullet holes with a little dark-haired boy in a torn, dirty maroon T-shirt, sitting beside him. Both are smiling at the camera, Cyrus's gun across their knees. Such a contrast in their looks – the child with his dark brown hair, almost black eyes and Mediterranean skin, and Cyrus with his freckles, blue eyes and sunburnt nose. He always had such an easy way with children – maybe it was his smile that made him irresistible to them.

There are photos of the desert in Afghanistan; incredibly beautiful mountains in the background and a young soldier aiming an enormous gun out across the land from the parapet walls – a big smile as he knew he was being photographed. In one of his letters Cyrus had written, *'If you could see what I'm looking at now you'd be pretty shocked, it's pretty stunning to be honest.'*

Looking through his photos, I can see what he means about the scenery. He also went on to say, *'I could probably sling-shot a stone from where we were last contacted (shot at) ha ha ha, pretty fucking scary, hey!'* What a reminder of how dangerous that country is – and their ability to smile and pose for a camera while on look-out for an enemy that is, probably, within easy range.

Then Cyrus bare-chested on a quad bike, laughing at the camera, surrounded by tents, men, equipment, and the dust that gives everything a slightly orange tinge. Soldiers sitting on the edge of vast poppy fields, looking relaxed – but I'm sure they are on full alert, aware of their surroundings and its dangers. Men lying on camp beds jammed together tightly, resting, waiting, smoking, writing letters home, reading and listening to iPods. They all look so young.

Somehow he had managed to set his camera up to take a photo of him and Elliott within a frame of a large blue heart, with 'love' written across it. The biggest grins on their faces, playing up to the camera – such great friends.

> *27th April – Afghanistan*
> *I've been thinking of loads of things and places to do, go and see. Me and Elliott are going to go to Amsterdam after this. I THINK WE MAY HAVE DESERVED IT!!*

Then my favourite photograph – one of him on his own, in what looks like a large wooden box, which I assume must be a gun turret, covered with camouflage netting, a gun on a tripod to his right. He's wearing his helmet and looking directly at the camera, giving it a 'thumbs up'. As always, he is smiling. I find myself kissing his face and then the tears start again. The emptiness returns and I don't know how I'll cope.

I've not written anything for a couple of weeks. Perhaps I thought I'd said all there was to say. Not so. If I share this with people, will they get even the slightest inkling as to how I feel – as to how Rob, Zac and Steely feel? Would it have the same effect as Cyrus's letters?

No, their impact was that fact that he was so young, yet able to write so beautifully and thoughtfully about us, and about what he would like us to be able to do. I don't think he fully understood the devastation his death would bring. I don't think he thought he was as important and vital to us as a family as he was. I know he knew he was loved, but I don't think he knew just how much he would be missed, and by how many people.

How can someone who didn't live here all the time, leave such a massive hole in our very being? Is it the fact that we will never hear his voice again – never again have to collect him from the airport or train station? Is it that we will never see those blue eyes, and hear his laugh or feel the pressure of his chest against us in a hug? It's all those things and so much more – so very much more.

I think the numbness is wearing off. I'm finding myself having more and more bad days. I thought that they would decrease, not increase, as time went on. It's the not sleeping and the nightmares that wear me down lately. I dream of him every night. Last night I dreamed that we were in Ireland and that the platoon was sitting in chairs in front of us, rather like they all used to do for the school class photo. Cyrus was there in the middle row, looking pale and his hair was all over the place, but he kept smiling at me, saying that it was all ok, that he would still get his medal. He was thin and slight, looked tired. I knew even in my dream that he was dead but he still kept smiling at me with tired blue eyes that had lost their sparkle. How can I be having conversations with the ghost of my dead son? Why is it him that's telling me everything will be ok? The face in my dream was the face I saw in the coffin – only this time his eyes were open. I used to think that people who talked to the dead were delusional, and now I find I'm right there among them.

Our neighbour has cut the bottom of the Russian vine that was growing in an oak in the hedgerow at the bottom of our gardens. It has died off now, but when the sun catches it, it is exactly the same colour as Cyrus's hair, red, golden and bronze, and maybe even a little dark brown or black. It's unruly too, just as his was in the coffin. He was so particular when it came to his hair that it seems strange, the last time I saw him, that he'd let it get that way. He would spend ages with gel and wax trying to get his barely two-centimetre-long hair looking perfect. He was very proud of his looks – took great care of himself. Our local hair-dresser would understandably shudder as he walked in, with his hair already short and immaculate, expecting a haircut he could leave the shop with that would make him look even better. She knew what he was like as they had known each other for years, he and her son were very good friends, and had been at secondary school together – he too was very meticulous about his appearance.

> *1st May 2009 – Afghanistan*
> *I think I've stopped burning, I'm slowly going brown and my hair is getting ridiculous – just wait till I come home I'll look like a fucking Wooky!*

I suppose when you're fighting a war it doesn't really seem relevant to make sure your hair looks good. Strange, but it makes me stop and catch my breath sometimes when I look out of the window at that vine. I feel the need to stuff my hands into my mouth again.

CHAPTER 6

WOOTTON BASSETT

When Cyrus last came home on leave he brought with him a pair of khaki shorts and an Op Herrick 2008/9 T-shirt with The Rifles insignia on the front, and on the back, in large black letters, the word 'Rifles' where a picture of a sniper rifle is used as the letter 'I'. Op Herrick is the codename under which all British operations in the war in Afghanistan have been conducted since 2002. The shorts he gave to Zac and the T-shirt to Rob. The first time Rob wore that T-shirt was the day after we were told Cyrus had been killed. He wore it for the newspaper photographs, he wore it when we went to Lyneham and he wore it when we went down to Wootton Bassett for the first time to join the masses and pay our respects on 16th June, when Lieutenant Paul Mervis of 2nd Battalion, The Rifles and Private Robert McLaren of The Black Watch, 3rd Battalion The Royal Regiment of Scotland were repatriated.

Captain Richard Sellars commented on the T-shirt when we first met him at the hotel the evening before

Cyrus was repatriated, and it was how he recognised us among the crowds of mourners that lined the streets in that small town in Wiltshire.

It seemed as though thousands of people had turned up – many different uniforms worn by young and old – Riflemen from 1 Rifles, soldiers from The Black Watch with their black uniforms, the British Legion with their standards, bikers who were ex-servicemen and women all in their leathers, covered in badges. It was almost a carnival atmosphere – but not quite, these are people who want to show their support and sorrow; this amazing town gives them the chance to do just that. All are there for one reason and one reason only – to pay their final respects to fallen heroes; to throw flowers, shed tears and pray for those lost and those families who were now lost.

It is moving stuff, here on the main road through a small town. People are gathered who are proud to be British – and acutely proud of these young men and women who have made the ultimate sacrifice, in order that they can continue to live in peace, in a democratic society without fear. These people of Wootton Bassett have been honoured by the Queen in recognition of their selfless actions. I wonder how much grief one town can witness without feeling the need to let others share the burden. I get the feeling that they do this with immense pride, and I thank them all for being there when Cyrus came home. What a magnificent gesture – what magnificent people. They too will be forever in my thoughts.

My tears that day were not just for the men in those coffins, but for the families that will be forever broken –

not able to hold their loved ones again, not able to share their lives with them. For all those whose faces are etched with the agony of loss – so many young people, people who do not really understand what they are witnessing, completely unable to comprehend why they are watching their brothers and friends coming home in boxes.

> *12th May 2009 – Afghanistan*
> *On some much sadder news, one of our Rifleman died a few days back, we had a parade and a few minutes' silence. It's so strange how many emotions you go through living in these conditions – its like everything wants to beat you and re-win your day. Its about not letting it get to you and don't worry nothing fucking gets to me. Well I'm off. I love you all loads and thanks for my parcels and letters. Lots of love xxx*

The bell tolled and all fell silent. I don't even remember hearing any birdsong – almost as though they know the significance of this. We stood with the Legion at the Memorial, craning our necks to catch a glimpse of the top-hatted procession leader walking in front of the cortege.

We could hear only-just-audible gasps and sobs as they came ever closer. My skin was covered in goose-bumps and my mouth took on its familiar dryness as my tears fell at the sight of the wave of complete misery coursing through the crowd. Then there they were – those hearses with their precious cargo, draped in Union Flags, the vehicles covered in roses thrown from the kerbside. It was almost unbearable. I felt as though I was being strangled. I don't know how much suffering one person can take.

I used to have a brain that worked, but now the door has shut and I can't find the way out. I forget things these days – mundane things, but not the painful things. The brain has a strange way of filing things away – all the painful thoughts are at the front, ready to jump out when you least expect it.

How am I? I wish I knew. I feel the need to write, and yet I'm not sure if it will lead anywhere or if it will ultimately help me – or anyone else for that matter. I just need to get the thoughts out of my head to relieve the pressure. If I write the words down, then they are preserved. If I just say them then they are gone once the sound stops. I know that even in this awfulness I don't want to lose them – I've lost too much already.

I don't really want to remember the horror of all this, but I do know that in the months to come I will re-read this and realise that I've come a long way – that hopefully I've not gone completely mad. How many women actually remember the *exact* pain of childbirth? We can't, or surely we would only ever have one child. So in a way, if I don't write this down, how will I know the exact pain of the death of a child? I don't want to remember the pain – it's just that I'm scared I'll forget.

For the past four years I have worked as the coordinator for Headway South Bucks, a small charity that runs a day centre and respite relief, in Bourne End Buckinghamshire, for people with acquired brain injuries, and their families and carers. One of our clients was a man from Sunderland called Kevin. He once told me the story of how he got his brain injury. He and some friends won an amount on the Lottery, but while out celebrating their win, a car mounted the pavement and Kevin was hit. He always used to say, 'Be careful what you wish for, hinney.' And at the time I thought how sad it was to have good luck one second, only for it to bring bad the next. I think I know what he meant now. Life needs to be lived here and now, not wishing for things to be different – money, job, friends – it takes its own twists and turns without you wishing to change it. If you do wish for change, it might not come in the form you'd hoped for.

I don't think I'd wished for a different life. I know now that if I had, for every action there is a reaction, and I suppose not always the one you want. Perhaps we lose those we love for a reason – those with religion would say it was 'God's will'. I don't believe that for a second, but I do wonder why Cyrus had to die so young, when there was so much more for him to achieve in this life.

We are all here for such a short time anyway, so I don't know why his time was cut shorter than others'. The unfairness of it all is overwhelming. I hate this lonely road, but I know I don't walk it alone – I share it with Rob, Zac and Steely.

We went to Wootton Bassett a second time on 14th July 2009, to pay our respects to the eight British soldiers who had been killed in a twenty-four-hour period in Afghanistan the week before. We stood in stunned silence as the eight coffins came past. The sorrow runs so deep, there are no words that can describe the sadness. Five of them were from 2nd Battalion, The Rifles: Corporal Jonathan Horne, Rifleman William

Aldridge, Rifleman James Backhouse, Rifleman Joseph Murphy and Rifleman Daniel Simpson; Rifleman Daniel Hume of 4th Battalion the Rifles, Private John Brackpool, Prince of Wales' Company, 1st Battalion Welsh Guards and Corporal Lee Scott of 2nd Royal Tank Regiment. All young, all with their whole lives ahead of them – all died doing a job they loved within the fold of a family far larger than ours. They had such courage – it was such a shame... such an awful way to welcome them home.

On November 10th Rob went to Wootton Bassett alone to pay his respects. Six more men, six more coffins. Warrant Officer Class 1 Darren Chant, Sergeant Matthew Telford and Guardsman Jimmy Major from the Grenadier Guards, Corporal Steven Boote and Corporal Nicholas Webster-Smith from the Royal Military Police and Serjeant Phillip Scott of 3rd Battalion, the Rifles. Six more soldiers who had paid the ultimate price.

I couldn't go with Rob as I had been asked to talk to the Year-11 students at Chiltern Edge, where Cyrus had spent – and not spent – his secondary school years. I talked about Cyrus and the fact that he'd not liked school. He had spent his last year attending school three days a week, and working two days a week tiling and building with Rob. This had all been allowed and approved by the school, as to get him to attend three days a week was seen to be better than him dropping out completely. The days with Rob were both very physical and educational, in their own way, but it seemed ridiculous that to have your own son work with you needed approval from Social Services, Health and Safety clearance, and liability insurances. Still, this arrangement helped Cyrus stay on track and take his GCSEs, as he needed them to join the Army. It was difficult to articulate to fifteen- and sixteen-year-olds how it feels to lose a son in this war – and also why I felt it was important that our troops were in Afghanistan, and how I believed we must support our forces. They are, after all, protecting us and our way of life.

The last time we went to Wootton Bassett was on Mothering Sunday, 2010 when, over seven hours, thousands of bikers rode through the town. Official figures claim that 10,500 were there, but I've heard it was more likely 15,000. It was so moving, these people from all over the country and some from abroad, here in Wootton Bassett, supporting our men. Where else, except the Cenotaph in London, do so many gather to show solidarity in grief and pride for both those who have died and those left injured? I was humbled by their charity. My hands were sore from clapping, I wanted to thank them personally, but of course that was impossible.

We've not been down since. It's not that I don't want to go for every single soldier that passes through, but my shoulders are not broad enough to carry the weight of all that grief. My heart has already been ruptured and it can't take any more.

I have heard that they are going to stop the repatriation ceremony at RAF Lyneham in 2011 and it will move to RAF Brize Norton in Oxfordshire. This will be a great pity as Wootton Bassett has become the country's focal point for the public to show their respect for our fallen heroes, and I don't think this could be replicated anywhere else.

CHAPTER 7

THE FUNERALS

We'd chosen our hymns – chosen the songs that meant most to us, decided on the prayers and Order of Service, been told about how the coffin would be moved from the hearse, how the Bearer Party would have to stop and duck to get through the main door of Reading Minster which is called the West Porch. It is low and narrow, so they would have to shuffle through with the coffin held at waist-height before lifting it on to their shoulders again, once they were inside. I didn't want to know any of these things. I didn't want to have to go into town and choose something to wear. Why should I have to pick an outfit to say goodbye to my most precious things? I'm losing my mind and my son at the same time.

Then deciding who will come in the cortege – who will sit in which car. Should we have a wake or just have those in the cortege come to the house beforehand and have coffee? Why am I worrying about old family feuds, what to wear, what time everyone will arrive and how on earth will we spend the night before?

In the event that was decided for us, because Maggie and her husband Fred had booked themselves into The Bull at Sonning, so they could be close for the next day. We went and had dinner with them. I am adopted and Maggie is my natural mother – so much shared and yet a life-time spent apart. We first met when I was seven months pregnant with Cyrus. Maggie had breast cancer and wanted to let me know that there was a possibility it was hereditary. Because mine was a private adoption she knew who my adoptive parents were, so tracking me down was not too difficult. It was peculiar, as I'd always been curious as to who my birth-mother was, and whether I replicated her in any way. I so wish it wasn't the way it turned out.

Five years after Maggie and I first met, their eldest son Simon died. He was taken from them as suddenly and unexpectedly as Cyrus was from us, due to a brain haemorrhage. So here I was, dealing her another cruel blow – she had lost a son and now a grandson. I'd never understood her pain, but I do now, and I'm sorry that I hadn't been able to give her the support she needed. Now here she was, being so brave and spending this evening with us, supporting us, empathising with us. It was an immense gesture of love – the ultimate maternal gesture.

I have always known I was adopted. Maggie worked as a nurse alongside my adoptive father, a neurosurgeon, in the north of England. He and his wife – she a doctor too – were unable to have children at that stage, and it seemed only natural for them to adopt me. My early years were full of love. My father moved us to the west coast of America for a couple of years before bringing us back to England where a brother, Sam, and six months later a sister, Hermione, (Mione) were adopted.

By now I felt that their work as doctors had become the focal point of their lives, even though two years after they adopted Sam and Mione they managed to have a natural son of their own, Ben, who was born in Glasgow. By the time Ben was two and I was eight, Dad had relocated us to Toronto in Canada, where we spent nearly four years.

We settled into life on a quiet suburban street, where all the front gardens were open, and as children we played with our friends across all the lawns. One Christmas I was given a golden retriever puppy. I named her Honey – and I loved her more than any friend. Together with the other neighbourhood children, I would ride up and down the gardens on my bike, with Honey running by my side.

I can see now, that this is where a shift in our family started – subtle changes, hushed arguments. My father began to spend more and more time at work, making it increasingly difficult to obtain and retain his love and attention. I adored him – possibly because he was so aloof, incredibly intelligent, difficult and distant. There were times when I wished I shared his genes – to be as clever as him, to have his drive.

Sam struggled with being adopted. He used to cry at night, and I'd hear him from my room and sneak down to the basement room that he and Ben shared. I would climb up on to the top bunk with him and listen to him as he wrestled with the unknown. Who was he? Where did he come from? Why was he different? Why didn't he fit in? Feelings of blame and rejection simmered under the surface, and I don't think I ever managed to reassure him. He is still full of self-doubt, disjointed and unable to fit in – not sure of his role in the world, as he is always wondering who his real parents are. I have never felt like that – I've always been self-assured, and confident in the person I am, rather than wondering about the person I might have been, should Maggie never have had to give me away.

One day, when I was eleven years old, I remember Dad coming home and asking me how quickly I could pack a suitcase, putting in only the things I really needed, as we were booked on a flight in the morning to leave Canada for England. I was devastated, Honey was not coming with us, and arrangements had already been made for somebody to collect her in the morning. I spent the night on the floor, under the dining room table with her, and to this day have never known what became of my beloved dog.

My mother, brothers, sister and I arrived at a little rented cottage in Bledington in the Cotswolds. My father didn't come with us – instead he flew to South Africa looking for work. Six months later we moved again as the lease had run out on the cottage, but it was only sixteen miles away to Stanton. By this time Dad was back in England, and had found work at the Maudsley Hospital in London.

By the end of the six-month lease in Stanton, he had bought a house in Henley-on-Thames, Oxfordshire. It was here, in Henley, that I was at my happiest. I made friends at school, had a part-time job in the local sweetshop, went to the youth club twice a week, and felt I had gained some kind of freedom and independence.

Life outside my family became very important, as Dad was rarely at home, and Mum had private patients in the house most evenings.

Rob and I got to know each other through school and the youth club. We became good friends and slowly a relationship developed. He was exciting – so different from anyone I'd ever met before. Our home lives were completely different – mine seemingly restricted, his free and full of wildlife. A crow called Grunt, a ferret called Jasper, a one-winged rook who lived in the shed at the side of his house and only came out for food or to chase the postman; guinea pigs, chickens, gerbils and a kestrel. He would catch slowworms during the summer and keep them in tanks. His garden and house reminded me of the TV programme 'Steptoe and Son', full of random sheds and part of an old Bedford van made into an aviary where Rob kept zebra-finches, budgies and canaries.

Rob would wake at dawn and walk for miles through the woods around Henley – he loved nature and wildlife. At weekends we would meet and Rob would teach me to ride his motorbike in the woods. Sometimes he would go night-fishing on the Thames with friends, and I would sneak out of my house, which was just a few streets from the river, to join them, making sure I was back in the morning before Mum noticed I was missing. He was not the sort of person my parents would have liked me to be with; they would have preferred an A-level student with the promise of a university place – instead I had fallen for a wild boy who rarely went to school, rode motorbikes and kept ferrets.

My happiness was short-lived. The summer before I turned sixteen I was told that once I'd finished my

O Levels we would be moving to Sydney, Australia where Dad had already set himself up with a job and, unbeknown to us, had also found a flat for, and installed his English girlfriend. The fact that Rob and I had already become a couple was not taken into consideration, nor were the feelings of the rest of the family; he made us move anyway. I was losing faith in him. My brothers and sister had been dispatched to boarding schools, and Mum and I were left to fend for ourselves (he left the family home three months after we arrived), in a country I had no wish to be in. I began to stop loving him. I was dreadfully unhappy.

After two and a half years in Sydney, Dad decided he wanted Ben to be educated in England, and once he had been accepted at Harrow, Mum returned with Sam and Mione (both aged fifteen), to start again. She bought a house in Cambridge so that she could be halfway between Ben in Harrow and Sam in Oundle, Peterborough. Mione went to the local comprehensive school. I, by this time, had left home and was living in a rented house, so was not included in this move back to England, and continued working as a secretary for another eighteen months. I saved enough money for a one-way ticket. This time the decision to move was mine. I took advantage of the fact that Mum was living in England, booked myself on a plane and moved in with her.

Rob and I had always kept in touch, even though we had both tried to move on, and had been involved in other relationships while I was in Australia. We were now both single and nervous and we took uncertain steps to see each other again. We had not been together for nearly four years. Rob came up to Cambridge and we went out for dinner. We have not spent more than a week apart since, and I cannot imagine my life without him.

I wonder now if it was the difficult – and eventually non-existent – relationship I had with my adoptive father that has been the reason I've never questioned who my natural father is. I know he was a doctor and that he was handsome and I am sure that Maggie would tell me more if I asked. Sadly, I have lived the past thirty years without the influence of a father-figure, and my children without their grandfather.

I need Maggie. She has given me balance – having met her I understand now why I am who I am. Why I have strawberry-blonde hair, blue-grey eyes and a blush of freckles over my skin. She gave me up through love and hoped it would give me the chance to be brought up within the stability of a family – something she could not offer herself at that stage of her life. Such an unselfish gesture, considering that she cared for me for the first six weeks of my life while she waited for my new parents to return from South Africa, where they had been working. I wonder if I could have been as brave.

For the morning of the funeral we thought it a good idea to display some of the numerous photos we'd taken of Cyrus over the years – giving us all a focal point rather than having to make polite conversation. There was nothing to say – we wouldn't want to talk.

Our dining room table is an old pine one and we've put a piece of toughened glass on the top. Between the table and the glass we put the photos of Cyrus. Cyrus as a baby, as a toddler, on holiday, with dreadful haircuts, at the school prom, with his brothers and friends; all of them painful to look at. In all of them he was smiling. That smile that used to end an argument, that got him out of trouble, that melted hearts, that made him friends, that lit up a room – the smile that breaks my heart every time I see it in a photograph, knowing that I'll never see it in the flesh again.

There were some photos that only we had seen. Now we shared them with the people whom we thought should be there before we had to leave and say our last goodbyes. Captured moments of a life that was too short – moments in the life of someone I will miss until I die.

Ian came dressed in uniform, waiting silently in the corner while we stood awkwardly, trying to have a conversation with our families. Rob's dad was making a fuss, insisting he should be in the car directly behind us in the cortege. Then there was my mother, taking photographs of Ian in his uniform, and the coffin inside the hearse – why would you want such an awful photograph? It was bizarre, odd people doing odd things and, we felt, behaving inappropriately.

Then it was time to go. Ian led us to the first car, which he got into with Rob, the boys and me. As we moved off, I noticed our postman standing to attention, and as we joined the main road a police escort appeared. All the lights were changed to green so that we wouldn't become a target, and so we could have a smooth ride to the Minster. I'd never thought of being a target. I suppose there are those out there who might have wished to do us harm – but the harm had already been done.

There was quite a crowd outside the Minster. I suppose Friday lunchtime was always going to be busy. We noticed two men in T-shirts and shorts, and both stood to attention. 'They have got to be soldiers,' Rob said. No uniforms though – not deemed politically correct I've been told; pity we can't be proud of our forces.

Inside, the Minster was full to bursting. Even the minstrel's gallery was overflowing. There were speakers outside too, so those in the street could hear the service. We were to wait and follow the coffin. When the Bearer Party lifted him, it seemed so effortless I wondered how heavy the coffin was. As they approached the West Porch they stopped, lowered the coffin then shuffled through the door, and lifted his coffin back on to their shoulders. R. Kelly's 'If I could turn back the hands of time' started and the intake of breath was audible from outside. We followed. The church was cold – or maybe it was just me. I tried to detach myself, as if I was in a dream. There were so many people – not an empty pew.

They gently lowered his coffin with its Union Flag, his cap, his belt and five white roses on to the stand at the end of the nave, in front of the choir stalls. The pulpit was on the left and we sat in the front pew on the right hand side. I have no idea what the order of service was – I just kept looking at the coffin, unable to take in the fact that he was lying in there. It looked so lonely – I wanted to hug it, put my hand on it, and tell him it was ok, we were here. I couldn't. I had to be brave. I had to be strong.

Major Mark Owen, whom we'd first met at the Hilton Hotel in Swindon, stood and talked about Cyrus's career in the Army, quoting from the eulogy written by Colonel Rob Thomson. They were words I'd read on the MoD site – words that meant so much and yet were meaningless because we'd lost him. Another soldier stood and read from a piece of paper. I didn't recognise him, and he seemed to be struggling to read the words. I thought that perhaps the writing was bad.

Then it was Steely's turn. Both he and Zac had written something on the night that we learned of Cyrus's death. I didn't know what they had written prior to this – it was just so courageous of them to stand in that church and say those words to Cyrus and the congregation. We'd told them before in the car that if they couldn't manage it, the Canon would read for them. 'No-one is going to read this but me. If I can't do it then they won't be heard,' Zac said through gritted teeth. He had also elected to read his piece last.

When the time came they both stood there, our boys, and read with such pride and in such clear voices, those last precious words to their brother, telling him how much he meant to them, how much they were going to miss him, how proud of him they were and how much they loved him.

Not a dry eye. Tissues being passed along and behind, noses being blown discreetly. So much pain – so many of the pews taken up by the young. No real comprehension of what was happening. I didn't cry, I just smiled at the coffin and thought that he would so liked to have seen this. A Minster full of family and friends, uniforms and pride. I knew the tears would come – but not here.

Then 'Ave Maria' sounded through the speakers and we stood, and followed his coffin out to the waiting hearse. The bell tolled and there was a slight cooling breeze on this warm June day. Captain Richard Sellars took my arm as we watched the Bearer Party slide the coffin into the back of the hearse. Captain Sellars – another nice man whom I wish I'd met under different circumstances. He helped us into the waiting car and then we were whisked away through the green lights towards the cemetery. I have no idea how long it took to get there. Shock had set in.

There is a small military graveyard at the cemetery, which is only a quarter of a mile from our house, and this is where our precious treasure was to be buried. I'd not even realised there was one there and I was surprised to learn that there are not these plots in every cemetery across the country. No-one had been buried there since the end of World War II, but now our son was going to join those who went before. The first to be buried there in over sixty years.

We walked behind him, through the corridor of the Firing Party. There, behind a low hedge, was a gash in the earth that would soon be filled with my flag-draped child. We stood inside the hedge, facing a sea of people; pale, weeping, crying, all dressed in black, and most wearing sunglasses. Some stood behind us, sobbing quietly into soggy tissues.

The prayers were said and slowly, so slowly, the Bearer Party folded the Union Flag almost as if they were performing a ballet, each movement precise, each movement making it smaller, each movement steeped in history and tradition. His cap and belt were removed from the top of the coffin, and they gently lowered him into the ground to the sound of gunfire. Even though I knew they were going to fire their weapons I jumped, as did everyone else. My heart completely broke and then I couldn't stop the tears.

Colonel Nick Parker, whom we'd first met at Lyneham, moved forward. I knew that he was going to give me the folded flag, cap and belt. 'Help me please. I don't think I can hold it on my own,' I whispered to Rob. He didn't catch what I was saying and I had to repeat it. He helped me lift my arms and together we received these items – the symbols of his job, symbols of his life and symbols of our loss.

The Canon then approached with a silver bowl which held some of the earth that had been removed during the digging of Cyrus's grave. He put my hand into it and led me towards the hole, telling me I must throw a handful on to the coffin. The hole was so deep, and he seemed so far away. I didn't want to do it but everyone was watching; it was so quiet, it was so final. The dirt landed with a thud, and I thought I might just jump in too, one more time to be close, one last moment. Rob and the boys came next, their handfuls on top of mine, then it seemed that the whole crowd moved as one and took a grain of earth, throwing it in together with dozens of roses. So many people came and hugged us – people I had not seen for years, people whose names I couldn't remember, faces I couldn't place.

There were other people there too – those we had asked to be told of his death, knowing they would want to pay their last respects. There were people who had only known him as a soldier, trained him – made him into a man. One of these was Corporal Pete Bevan, whom we'd first met at an open day in Bassingbourn, twelve weeks after we had left Cyrus waiting at the bus stop, at the start of his basic training. The second time we met Corporal Bevan was at Cyrus's Passing Off Parade, when we had spent a long time talking to him and Captain Emily Stokes, realising that they had a lot a respect for each other not just as soldiers, but as people. I don't know how often training personnel and trainees become friends, but I'm sure had Cyrus lived they would have kept in touch. We had asked Richard Sellars if they both could be contacted. Captain Emily Porter was on tour in Afghanistan when she heard of Cyrus's death; we received a letter from her.

FMCC

JFSp (A)

Op HERRICK 10

09 Jun 09

Dear Mr and Mrs Thatcher,

I wish to express my condolences at this immensely difficult time. Having had the great honour to have been your son's Platoon commander during his basic training at ATR Bassingbourn, I know that his loss will be sorely felt by all who had the pleasure in knowing him.

In all the time I served at ATR Bassingbourn, your son Cyrus has remained in my memory as the greatest of characters, with his extremely infectious enthusiasm and cheery demeanour, no matter how bad the weather or how arduous the task in hand. He never failed to lift the spirits of all those around him and was one of the most considerate young men I have ever had the pleasure to meet. Always completely dedicated,

> *he had the admirable ability to take everything into his stride, making him a fine example to all others. His love of you all was in much evidence and I believe this helped make him the exceptional young man that he was.*
>
> *I realise my words cannot ease the pain you are all feeling, but I hope that in knowing others' thoughts are with you, it may go some way to helping ease some of your sorrow.*
>
> *With sincere regards*
> *Emily*
> *Capt EJ Porter (nee Stokes).*

We were touched and honoured that she was able to attend.

We had also asked if Serjeant Leon Smith (Smudge); who had been injured by the explosion that killed Cyrus, and was here in England receiving treatment, would be able to speak at the service on behalf of 10 Platoon, as he had been the Section Leader on the day. We'd been told by the Army this might not be possible due to his injuries and state of mind, given the subsequent injuries and losses suffered by 10 Platoon.

Captain Richard Sellars led us towards the soldier who had spoken at the Minster, and introduced him to us. He was Serjeant Smith, so now it made sense – why he had struggled with the words in the church. They were his words; he had been there, had seen it all. He had stepped up to the mark, done it, and despite his own pain he had decided to honour our son, his platoon and all those who couldn't be here. In typical 'soldier' style, he hadn't shied away from what must have been a harrowing ordeal. He did so well to keep in control. Pain was etched into his face – the agony of having to meet us like this, to see one of his men laid to rest, to know about Paul – and to be here safe when his men were still out there, still having to face the fear of the unknown, and the fear of the known. We embraced and thanked him for being there, embarrassed that we'd not known who he was earlier. He just smiled his shy, sad smile and I felt a huge affection for him.

I'm not sure what happened next. Everything was a tear-streaked blur. I only remember being helped back into the car and driven home. We'd asked everyone who had met at the house earlier to come, collect their cars and go. We had decided against a wake (the boys' friends had already been to see us and toast Cyrus), and didn't want lots of people drinking, eating, and talking about times gone past mixed in with laughter and plans for the future. What is our future? How do we plan? Why should I laugh? How dare they? No, that's not fair – our pain is different from theirs, but they can go home and get on with their lives. We have to learn how to live our new one.

I think by the evening most of the local pubs had kicked out the funeral rabble and run out of Sambuca. I'm glad for them – that they held their own wake and had the opportunity to be together in their sorrow. I didn't have the energy to host one, and I've always thought they were ever so slightly disrespectful.

I wanted a cigarette. I've not smoked since I was twenty-five, but right then I could have demolished a whole packet. I didn't, I knew it was just a feeling that would pass, but the thought was comforting for a moment. I lay on the bed and slept. What do we do now?

Five days later, Rob and I summoned the strength to go to Paul Mervis's funeral. I'm sure I saw the Mervises in the Minster, but my mind plays tricks. Later, in a letter, his mother Margaret said, 'If only we could turn back the hands of time,' and then I knew they had been there for Cyrus. It's strange that we felt the need to go to this funeral – not to witness the pain of others but from the urge to show just how much this man we'd never met meant to us. We went for the Platoon, we went for Cyrus, we went for ourselves and we went for Paul's family. Part of me is glad that Cyrus never had to witness this awfulness; he will never know the agony of having to say goodbye to a loved one.

We had to walk down a steep path towards the graveside at Aldershot Military Graveyard and the soldiers' steel-capped shoes slipped – it was easier to walk on the grass. The cemetery was huge, beautifully kept, peaceful – but again not somewhere I wanted to be. It was not how I wanted to meet Paul and his family. We had been so desperate to meet this man when we got his letter. He was the connection to Cyrus and this whole war – and now here we were, attending his funeral.

It was to be a Jewish ceremony and the men were asked to wear a small black kippah. No flowers – only poems and prayers read by his brother and sister, eulogies from friends and colleagues. Different service, different place, different people – same outcome.

Before the ceremony we were introduced to a pale young man in a wheelchair. His name was Matt Wilson (Willo), who like Cyrus was part of C Company 10

Platoon under Paul's command and the Sunday after Cyrus was killed he had his leg blown off at the knee while on patrol. Because he was so heavily sedated due to his injuries, he had been unable to attend Cyrus's funeral, but he had recovered sufficiently and had insisted he be allowed out of hospital for the day to attend Paul's. He still had dried blood on his hands and under his fingernails. He looked so small and white – a ghost of a man, so young to face death and mutilation. His eyes filled with tears when he took my hand and said how sorry he was about Thatch. Amazing, these men who become soldiers.

What the hell was I supposed to say to him? His mum was with him, and we both cried for Cyrus, for Paul and for Matt. She had already given so much; her husband – a soldier too – was killed in a blast in Northern Ireland when Matt was four years old. Surely this is too much pain for one family to take.

Serjeant Leon Smith was there too. He had tears in his eyes. He said he would always blame himself for Cyrus's death, and said it should have been him instead. I told him that there was no blame to be had. We would *never* blame him or anyone else. Cyrus did exactly what he wanted to do, and if his orders were to be at that place at that time, then he followed them to the letter, as any soldier would have done.

Leon has the agony of having to live with the vision of what happened, while I only have to live with the picture I've painted in my head. I don't know if I could cope with the real thing. Leon was still waiting to hear from Selly Oak Hospital about his hearing tests. His hearing had been damaged by the blast and unless the doctors thought it was up to scratch, he wasn't going to be allowed to return to Afghanistan. I think that was frustrating him. He felt completely useless here when his men were still out there fighting and trying to cope without him, Paul, Matt and Cyrus. I don't know if anyone else was injured from 10 Platoon after Cyrus and Paul were killed – we don't get that information. No-one does, but I think we should know – I'd like to be able to go and visit these men in hospital and tell them how brave I think they are, and that I think about them every day. I think we were deliberately kept away and, looking back, it makes sense. For all our good intentions, the parents of the dead visiting the living was probably not the best thing for them.

Grief and glue, sombre men and women in black standing on the grass watching as Paul was lowered into the ground. That was the point at which I had felt my heart break the Friday before, when we too had had to watch as Cyrus was lowered into the cold earth. So many people had thrown roses on Cyrus's coffin – so many young people constricted by grief, haunted by the process of saying goodbye to a much-loved friend, and not really comprehending the enormity of it all.

Parents and siblings having to say goodbye, consumed by choking glue and burning eyes – what could I say that didn't sound hollow? In the end, I went up to Margaret when we were in the Officers' Mess for the wake, and held her hand. She knew exactly what I was wanted to say without me having to utter a word. 'After all,' she whispered, 'you are the only person in this room who knows how I truly feel.' Yes, I understood – but I wished I didn't.

We met some of the wives – young girls with sadness and worry in their eyes. Their men were still out there; they have to go through the agony of hearing reports and hoping that it's not their man. They have young children and I worry for them all. I too am scared that I will recognise a name. I dread the phone ringing at odd hours just in case it is someone Cyrus was especially close to. I don't know if any of them are injured and in hospital somewhere. I wish I knew, so I could write and tell them I'm thinking of them.

If you look up 'grief' in a thesaurus there are nineteen other words of similar meaning. No one word can capture it, though. You can't trap grief in a word. None, in fact, is completely accurate, because grief changes – the grief I felt an hour ago is different from the grief I'm facing now, and it's no good trying to get used to the grief I feel today, as I know it will be a different grief tomorrow – but they all form part of how I feel.

I don't know if I had a timescale in mind when I might start to feel a part of my new life. Today, only ten weeks on, and yet I seem to have been at this point in time for years. Some days are definitely worse than others; they are all awful, but some more so than others.

I don't want people's pity. I can't have their under-standing because they don't understand. I'm not really sure what I want from friends and family. Just a second of their time – not too much or it becomes too hard to cope with. Just enough to skim across a thought or touch lightly on a phrase. Rather like being visited in hospital. You want to see people, but only for long enough to know that they have been – not long enough to have to talk to them. Does that make sense? Again, my head is playing tricks. I know what I'm thinking but when I write it down it comes out wrong. Maybe one day these words will make sense – dreams and glue bound together in confusion and wretchedness.

Wretched is a good word. Retch is what I want to do every time I think about the fact that I will never see Cyrus again. Along with scream and pull my hair, plunge a knife into my heart –blow my brains out. Of course I'll never do any of these things.

I have a picture in my mind of the last time I saw him. He was standing on the brick pier of the steps at the front of our house, waving. We had taken him to Heathrow Airport the day before, and prepared our goodbyes, only to discover his flight times had been changed, and he wouldn't be flying back to Belfast until the next day. This was great in one way, as it meant we had another night with him, but not so good in another, as the timing clashed with an appointment I had to attend with Zac. It was Rob who would take him back to the airport. So we have separate memories of the last time we saw him – mine are connected with him waving goodbye from the top of the steps, while Rob's with dropping him off at Heathrow Airport and sharing a last cigarette. Rob had given up smoking when he was thirty-one, so it was only when Zac and Cyrus started to smoke that he would occasionally have the odd puff. When Cyrus was home on leave he would stand at the back door and say 'Tab?' and Rob would follow him out to sit at the table on the decking, and share a cigarette and a shot of Sambuca. It is a ritual he still shares with Zac – I know it holds memories for them both.

That day he was wearing his favourite baby-blue jumper and jeans. He was tall, slender and handsome – so full of life. His broad grin showed off his straight white teeth – he still wore his retainer at night, having worn braces for so long he wasn't prepared to let his teeth get crooked again. His hair short and neat, ready for action. I wonder if he'd already decided his hair would not be cut again until his return home on leave, from Afghanistan, in July.

I wonder if you can run out of tears. I ask myself all these stupid questions over and over again. It is all so exhausting. My feet feel like lead, and my brain won't work properly. I can't be bothered to do anything – everything is an effort and yet I need to keep myself doing something or I'll go insane. Having too much time to think isn't a good thing.

CHAPTER 8

FIVE BOXES

The Army told us they would send back his belongings. I can't remember at what point they arrived – Ian brought them for us in a white van. Five large cardboard boxes. Was this what his life had amounted to? Nineteen and a half years – five large cardboard boxes? We lifted them gingerly into the front room. We now couldn't move because of them; our front room is quite small, and they filled it.

The first one we opened contained his double duvet and pillows. They went straight in the car, destined for the tip. Steely, Rob and I worked our way through the others. At one point I had to leave the room and Rob got cross – not really with me, but just with the horror of the whole situation. 'Don't you dare walk away and turn your back on him. What makes you think I can do this, when you don't think you can?' He was right. I came back in and we started again.

One box contained his Henry Hoover. I remember when he phoned and told me that he'd bought it. Here I am, crying over a fucking Hoover and ticking it off the inventory list. His shoes and socks went into the car, together with other pieces of clothing that we knew no-one would wear or want to keep for sentimental reasons.

He loved clothes, always making an effort to look 'just right' – even wearing a different aftershave each side of his face because he wanted to smell nice. Before he joined the Army it would be all about brand names and appearance, which would frustrate Rob as an avid outdoor-pursuits-man who believes the way to go is hardwearing, warm, dry and practical. He's right, of course, because you can't climb mountains, go down caves and kayak in a pair of Armani jeans.

The boys would always rib their dad about how he looked and dressed while on the many adventures he took them on. There was the day-sack, kitted out as though an Arctic expedition was imminent, and a survival kit that would have kept us all alive for months should we ever be stranded on a deserted island. These items came along first and foremost wherever we went, be it a two week holiday or a walk in the woods.

Whenever we arrived anywhere on holiday, I would find myself scanning the horizon, knowing that the highest point, at some stage, would have to be scaled – undertaken at first light as though it were a full-scale military operation. There were always groans from the boys and me, but every expedition would be a true adventure, and thoroughly enjoyed.

Amazing the change the Army made – there was clothing and equipment in those boxes that Rob would love to have had with us on those adventures.

All sorts of other things went into the car for their final journey to the tip. His bed, old bits and pieces that he'd kept for one reason or another, but didn't make sense to us, and which therefore it seemed pointless to keep them. Even, as extreme as it seems, all the stud walls from his room went out alongside the shoes and socks. Steely was struggling to sleep having to walk past his room every night, so the walls came down, and now he has one huge room that is void of Cyrus, yet so much of him is still there as part of it.

We didn't want his old room to become a shrine – how do you ever move forward if you keep it 'as it was'? He didn't live here any more, he just came home every so often, and slept in his old room, under his old duvet, talking to his brother through the wall – sharing secrets. A shrine would have been too painful to walk past. Would I leave the blind closed, or should I open it to make it not all seem so scary and depressing? No, we wouldn't use his room as a shrine.

We have a wooden trunk in the front room underneath his army photos and framed medals – that's our shrine. It's one that we can take with us, if we ever leave this house. It's one that isn't scary or dark. It's one that I still can't look at without wondering how we managed to put his life into such a small box. It's one that makes me cry.

Inside this trunk are the things that his soldier's life was about. His beret, his medals, his belt, his dog-tags and the carefully folded flag that was draped over his coffin. All the cards and letters we got are in shoeboxes in there too. The only thing that we haven't managed to look at is the poncho on which he was carried off the battlefield.

The soldiers of C Company wrote messages on it, but I can't bear to look – it's just too painful. How the hell do you write on a blood-covered poncho that you've carried your dead friend in? How brave are these men? How wonderful and caring? I will love them all for that for the rest of my days – I just wish they knew how much it means to us that they took the time to say goodbye.

It's all the little things that you don't think about in everyday life that suddenly become huge. His driving licence, his Army ID, his passport, chequebooks, and hole-in-the-wall cards – all came back with holes punched through them. It all seemed so final, so cruel. Their punching a hole through these things makes him a non-person now. How can this be? How does my son become a punched hole? He used to breathe and laugh, now he is just a hole – a hole in my heart, a hole in my family, a hole in my life, and a hole in a driving licence. Bloody hell.

Debbie, a friend of mine from schooldays in Henley, whose children both went to Chiltern Edge with the boys, said that she could see a change in my face. I know my inside has changed, but I'm not sure about the outside. Do I look older – I'm nearly fifty now. Am I paler, more drawn? Are these the changes she sees?

I don't want to look in the mirror – it's too honest. Looking at my own image is torturous because I know *he* will never see it again. My reflection only compounds the truth. Never again will my eyes see his face, my mouth feel the softness of his cheek or form words of love, and smile at the sound of his voice. Spiteful pain has taken everything from me, right down to being able to look at my own face.

All I see is him; the shared freckles across skin that is fair but has a sun-kissed blush. Even though he shaved, as the Army insisted on it, his face was smooth and child-like in its softness. It never acquired that 'rugged look'. I see our almond-shaped eyes – his so expressive. I could tell immediately how he felt, if he was angry, sad, drunk or happy – they spoke volumes. The paleness of our eyelashes – but his so long most women would kill for them; the arch of our lips. It has dulled my vision. I look but I'm not truly there – only the ghost of a child and the wasteland of my soul, a blurred reflection of the mother I once was. There are just shapes and colours, snatched at with furtive side-long glances, as to look openly would be too hurtful, too cruel, and too much a reminder of what I no longer possess. He will never gaze upon my face, and watch time change the lines, deepening some and softening others. That realisation becomes too personal even for me. His death has taken this from both of us.

Some people go grey overnight. I've just gone grey inside. Some people's hair falls out. I'm falling out of control. I worry that Zac and Steely will feel pushed out by my grief. I don't want them to think that I think only of Cyrus all the time – because that's not true. I can't stop thinking about him, but I think of them too. I know that I need to surround myself by the living, but leaving the dead behind is not an option right now.

I love my children differently. I always have, because they are different people, and deserve to be treated differently. I don't love any one child more than the other. I love them all equally, but I'm frightened they might not see it that way at the moment.

How can a parent love one above the other? If I decided to end it all tonight, surely that would signal to them that I loved them less – that their lives were insignificant in comparison – and that is not the case. That would be the ultimate betrayal of a mother's love, to love one more than another. I'm not that sort of person, not that sort of mother, not that sort of partner to Rob. They deserve all of me, and that is exactly what they will get until the day I die.

How is it that you can love someone who is no longer here? How is it possible to have that love? I have no control over this feeling of love. I understand 'falling in love' – but this is a different love. Yes, I fell in love with my children as they were born, so I guess there is no reason not to still have that rush of love, no matter how crippling, when they die. It is the power of this love that is so frightening.

I wish I were the sort of person who kept a diary. It would certainly make writing this much easier. I would be able to make sense of the days – put them into some sort of chronological order – but I'm not, and so this appears disjointed, which I find frustrating. I would like it to read smoothly and make sense, but it seems to jump all over the place, and I confuse myself re-reading it. Everything jumps, one thought to another, reliving all the horror of what has happened – jumping from one time to another, and not being able to differentiate between them.

Someone told me that it was natural for everything to seem so all over the place. Believe me, there is nothing natural about any of this. It is the most unnatural thing that I have ever experienced, and that's scary. I'm used to having some sort of control of my life, but now there is no control. I can't gauge how I'm going to feel or respond to people when they ask how I am.

Will I forget what he smelt like? Will I forget the feel of the pressure of his hug? The sound of his voice? I hope not, but I know time makes you forget. I never want to forget any of these things, and yet I don't really want to remember the pain – but they have to go hand in hand.

You can look at a photograph and know who that person was but you can't <u>feel</u> what they were like by looking at it – and that's what I'm worried I will lose with time. I don't want to lose the essence of him, and yet that is what this agony is all about– his essence that is now under six feet of orange earth and pots of colourful flowers and flickering candles.

I asked for a lock of his hair. I have it in a box, but I want to buy a locket and wear it around my neck. Is that morbid? I just want to know that he will always be close, and I couldn't think of any other way of doing it. I guess some people might find it a bit weird, but I don't really care what other people think. He was *my* son, so I will keep him close. I guess it's quite a Victorian thing to do… I wonder if he would be horrified. No – he'd probably just think I'd gone mad, and that it was all a bit freaky. He might also be quite flattered that I would want to keep him near. Who knows?

I used to be part of a fifth, and now I'm only a quarter. It's not a natural way for me to be – none of this is natural. I've watched programmes recently about parents who have lost children, and they all have that haunted look about them, I wonder if I look the same. None of them really understands what has happened, and seem to slog endlessly on with their lives, not completely knowing what they are doing or where they are going. I've joined this group. I feel listless, my feet are heavy and I find it hard to look at myself in the mirror – to see if I'm still really here. Some days I wish I were somewhere else – or someone else. Let somebody else take this pain and sadness, leaving me free as I was before, free of this tear-stained face and dry mouth

Because I am adopted, one of the most important things in my life was to become a mother and have children of my own. This was partly because I wanted someone who looked like me, or at least had some similarity to me, and partly because I felt that I had something I could give a child – or maybe even three.

I didn't pick up any spectacular parenting skills from my adoptive parents. They were/are doctors and had careers to pursue and patients to cure. I felt we were trophy children really, to be presented and talked about but only when convenient, left in the care of au pairs who were not much older than I was when I was a teenager. They didn't speak my language and I had no interest in them. Odd, to think that my childhood was influenced by strangers – girls away from home in a confusing distant land, where their emotions were not taken into consideration. They were paid to look after us, cook, clean, stand on the side of cold football pitches, and be there for us when our parents weren't.

I would have loved a mother who made cakes, and was at home when I got in from school. In Henley I had a school friend, Julie Callander, and that's what her mother did. I was so envious. Instead, we were met at the door by foreigners.

What I did get from my parents was the determination not to bring my children up the same way; our children were, and are the most important part of our lives. Everything we did revolved around them, and we overindulged them with time and love. We have had some of the best holidays, some in far-off and even exotic places. We've skied the Rockies, climbed in and out of pools of volcanic mud in Turkey, snorkelled in the Red Sea, driven quad bikes in the desert, waded through freezing streams in Wales, and the boys have all been caving. They've learnt how to water-ski, jumped out of aeroplanes and ridden on elephants in the jungles of Goa. They've swum in the warm waters of the Bahamas, and made sandcastles on deserted beaches. We've been crabbing and fishing for mackerel, skimming stones on Scottish lochs, searched for the fabled monster, clambered over ancient ruins, and made friends with newly-hatched turtles and world-weary tortoises.

I would spend hours reading them stories when they were small, making some up, and retelling favourites. I'd make costumes for school plays, painting faces while Rob made swords and shields from plywood, taught them to swim and shoot air rifles, how to kick-start motorbikes and have apple fights on tractor mowers. All these things we did with our children, watching them grow and learn – watching them smile and bloom, and hearing them laugh.

How can it be that we did so much for our children and yet we've now lost one? There are so many parents out there who can't wait for their children to become independent so that they can get on with their own lives. We've always lived *for* our children, and yet we're the ones who have been left with this gap in our family.

I know that both Rob's dad and my mother think that we've spoilt them, and spent too much money and time on them – but 'the proof is in the pudding' as they say, and I'm not sorry about a single penny that was spent, or a second of that time. I know in my heart that Cyrus went to war having experienced things many of his friends and peers never will, and I'm so glad that we had the opportunity to share all these things with our children.

Rob gets motion sick, but he still took his children to Disney World twice. Cyrus got motion sick – but he still got on the rides, was sick all the way up the slopes on the chairlifts in Canada. He tried scuba diving and even got thrown out of an aeroplane; he had the chance to try all of these things, and I'll never regret a single day of it. I'd even carry his vomit in a bag, day after day, if it meant that I could have him back here again. I've lost count of the days I carried those bloody bags.

Life is too short, however you look at it. He crammed in as much as he could, and I hope that Zac and Steely keep cramming. They have got such a lot to discover in this world, and need to take life by the scruff of the neck and swing it around a bit to see how it feels.

I'm afraid that I might become too over-protective of them. I don't want to smother them, but I can't help but worry. Steely feels it more than Zac, I think, yet I hope he still needs me. You can't switch off how you feel about your children, and as I keep telling him, he will always be my baby and nothing can change that. I have to learn to accept that they have grown up, and one day will have families of their own. Is it that I care too much? Will I stifle them and prevent them from growing straight and strong on their own? I hope not, but I know that I'll never be the mother to them I was before Cyrus was killed. That person has gone forever.

I do feel, though, that our parents should make more of an effort – or is that just me being selfish and bloody-minded? It makes me angry, because I know that if any of my children were going through this I would be on the phone every other day, even if only to say I was thinking of them. I can't help but compare – but as I said, we are different types of parents from our own, and this is our hell, not theirs. They've not been here, not experienced this, so who am I to judge them when the only way to really understand it is to live it?

Rob's dad won't let anyone talk about Cyrus. How stupid is that? Is he not proud of his grandson, and does he not think that he is worth talking about? I can't really get my head around the way his dad thinks. I told him he <u>should</u> talk about him – or else he might as well not have existed. I don't think he understood what I was trying to say, and I know that he is still cross with me for saying it, but I hope that one day he will understand, no matter how firmly he is set in his ways.

He is still a huge part of Rob's life, and even though I find him frustrating, I know that Rob will stand by him, as I know deep down that his dad <u>is</u> there for us. It would be nice though, if his dad could tell him every now and then. If questioned, his reason for not doing this is because he assumes we already know he's thinking of us, and that he's there for us – therefore there is no reason to tell us. So this, coupled with leaving us alone until we feel we're 'better and ready' is impossible to understand. What does one class as 'better'? As 'ready' as Rob gets, is biting the bullet and phoning, knowing that he can't discuss how he feels, and has to avoid any mention of Cyrus – such a shame, but his dad simply can't deal with it.

I know that people don't know what to say to us, that they are afraid they will upset us. Believe me, unless someone told me Rob or the boys had been killed, NOTHING would ever hurt as much as this. No-one can say anything that will distress me as much as this situation we all find ourselves in now.

I'm jumping again. I need to keep a notebook with me so I can write down things as I think of them. I don't want to forget what I think, and sometimes I have to try to retrace my steps so I can get my train of thought back again.

Sometimes it's hard to behave normally around Rob and the boys when everything is so abnormal. I try to paint on a face for them, but it doesn't always work. They see through my mask. I hate it, this new life. I'm not the person I wish I was – I just feel selfish. At times I don't want to share anything with anyone. I want to curl up and leave the pain behind and be by myself sometimes – but know that they are there when I need them. There are times, like now, when I think it would be easier to be on my own.

CHAPTER 9

SUMMER AND FORMS

I don't know if I will ever, over the years, get to the place that others reach – the place that allows you to move forward without the constant stabbing pain in your head and chest.

Everything seems duller now. Colours have faded and sounds are muted. Zac talked to me last night, and told me it was time I followed my own advice, and talked to friends and family. I don't think he realises that I do talk, but I don't go out much. I never really did before all this happened. Rob and I are private people, and we like our own company and that of our children. Insular, boring, un-sociable – no not really – just content with our lot... or we were.

It's not that we don't want to talk or see people – but everything is such an effort. Picking up the phone and talking to anyone is hard, as I find myself having to soothe them and their feelings. Why should I? We are the ones who have suffered most, as it is we who knew him the best and were interested in every single aspect of his life. They have their own lives, so why should I expect them to feel as I do? I don't like to keep on about his death, in case I bore people too much. Just because I think about it constantly doesn't mean that everyone wants to – and he was our son, so why should they?

However, it is a very lonely road, and some support from a parent would be nice once in a while. But I know that's not going to happen, because they don't understand how much it means, to have that crutch – that bolster. I'm the sort of person who needs to be told that I'm loved every so often. I have always told my children I love them. I hope they take that with them, and when they have children of their own, make sure their children know they are loved too.

I've changed. I know that I'm not the same person I was on 1st June 2009. My outlook on life has shifted. Things that I used to think were important simply aren't any more. All my edges are jagged. I've lost the ability to smile properly, and feel the warmth of contentment. I get a strange out-of-body feeling sometimes, looking at the world as if I were in a glass bubble, not quite able to catch the gist of conversations or the smell of flowers – like listening to conversations through a glass on a wall.

Some days I've loads of motivation, and I tell myself that I'm going to do all sorts of things – and sometimes I even manage to achieve them. Other days even breathing is an effort. I feel as though I've been in a freezer – my fingers don't work, my brain won't function, icy cold seeps through my very being. I go through the motions of work because I know I'd go mad if I were to sit at home all day. But there are certain aspects of it that I can't do, and I can't put a finger on what they are.

There are all the things that go with death that I'd not really appreciated, such as wills, probate, the Elizabeth Cross – and so many forms to fill in. Everyone asks the same heart-wrenching, gut-twisting questions: date of death, age at death, cause of death. Surely death is death. There seems so little compassion to these questions. Why do the 'whys' and 'wherefores' matter? The answer is always the same – he's dead. It's hard enough thinking about it, let alone having to write it down all the time.

How the hell am I supposed to fill in a probate form when I don't even know what day it is? This is what I do – paperwork. Rob does the physical work, while I do the bookwork. I was convinced I'd done it, and couldn't understand why it was taking so long to hear from the court, so when I looked in the briefcase to get the phone number I realised that I'd not even filled in the probate form. Well, thinking about it rationally, of course I'd not filled it in. I move in a daze most of the time, so what the hell I was thinking, I don't know.

It is the most complicated form I've had to complete. Everything has to be cross-referenced. I had to find out all his assets – well, what money he had in the bank and building society as he didn't have a house or major property. I had to make sure all the 't's were crossed and that I'd dotted all the 'i's, but because of the tears it was all I could do to see the pages clearly, let alone know if I'd done it properly. He was only nineteen, I shouldn't be filling in probate forms – he should be here, not dead.

We have to go to court tomorrow, to get the Grant of Execution; then we can start the unenviable job of moving his money around, sorting out what to do with it. I don't want it – I just want him. He was supposed to come home, not be a number on a probate form and a sum of money moving from one account to another. I hate it all.

I know that it's another 'first' that we have to overcome, and that this time next year we won't have to do this again, but it is all so difficult and mind-numbingly painful. There are going to be some horrible 'firsts' over the next few months, but I know we will get through them somehow. We are strong, but sometimes summoning up that strength is all too much. My days are sadder, and there is no respite from it – nothing I do stops the thoughts from seeping through.

These days I find myself not being able to look people in the eye. I'm afraid I will see their pity, and I'm also afraid they will be able to see into the pool of sorrow that lies behind my own eyes. I used to be able to look at people and have a direct conversation with their eyes; I've lost that. It is all too personal, and I can't share that with anyone yet. I honestly don't know if I will ever be able to. There are so many dark and secret places in my head these days, that are too painful to share.

Everything seems to be conspiring against me at the moment. My heart feels one thing, but my head tells me to feel another. I'm all mixed up, and not sure which way is up or down. I'm cold all the time. Loneliness is cold and I do feel lonely, and although I know there are people I can talk to or cry at, I still feel as though I'm on top of a mountain, and no one else is there. It's a bit like being in a glass tunnel. With the exception of Rob and the boys, everyone around me is carrying on as if nothing has happened. I know that it hasn't happened to them, but it did affect them in the beginning. It seems that they have moved on while we've stayed still. Of course they have moved on, and it's wrong of me to expect them to feel as we do, but it is a very surreal feeling.

I need to regroup my feelings and try to look at life differently now. I know exactly what Cyrus would want, and what he would say if he could, but it's very different physically trying to do it. It's the fact that I choke on it every time I think of him.

It's the 'NEVER' that is so difficult to come to terms with. How can it be that we will never see him again, hear his voice, touch his face, pick up his clothes, make his bed? How can it be? Yes, the 'never' is the hardest thing.

I hope that Cyrus didn't feel his death. I hope instant *is* instant, and that it was just as if someone had turned off a light. It would add to the horror if I knew that he had suffered. I hope he wasn't afraid and, that if he knows he's dead, he's not frightened. No more pain, no more suffering, no more tears or heartache. He'll never grow old or have worries – but then again I'll never be able to hold him. It's our 'never' that hurts.

When you look out through double-glazing at the wind blowing the trees and cars going past, you can't hear any sound, and that's what grief feels like today. I'm screaming in my head, but no sound comes out. All the emotions are there – just not the sound. I feel impotent and nothing I do produces anything other than the same sadness. The incapacity to help is frustrating and also very sad. 'Sad' is another word I've had to come to real terms with. Before it was just something one felt occasionally, now it's something I live with, constantly sitting on my chest weighing me down.

On 22nd August, Captain Richard Sellars, whom we'd not seen since he helped organise Cyrus's funeral, died in a hotel room of a heart attack. How fucked-up is that? He was such a nice man and he was so good to us, arranging Cyrus's funeral et al. He'd just finished his posting in Northern Ireland and was due to start a new one on the mainland. I know people die every day – but not people I know and like, not in my life. That's not what I saw my future being; death and all the horrors and nightmares that it brings. We are not able to go to his funeral, but I intend to write to his children and tell them what I'm sure they already know – that their dad was a really decent bloke and I'm going to miss him. I know we are in a bad place because under different circumstances, there is no way that we would not have gone to pay our last respects to this caring man.

I'm exhausted by all this death. It was never personal before. People died and I gave them a cursory thought, then moved on with whatever I was doing. Now every soldier is a son and it hurts all over again. Glue returns on a regular basis. I thought I'd managed to extract myself from it, but I guess it was just waiting, biding its time until I wasn't ready, and then it slowly crept back in, like smoke through my veins. It's silent and cunning, lurking at the back of the room, sneering at me when I think I've rid myself of it. I don't suppose it will ever truly go – glue is sorrow, pain and anguish, and those are things that I now have in my life. I wonder if it is true that you get used to it – that it becomes your new norm. As I said before, I was happy with the norm I had before, I certainly don't want to have to learn to live a new life.

It's all the little things that go to make a shitty day. Letters that need to be written to the Joint Casualty and Compassionate Centre (JCCC) about Cyrus's wages, having to enclose probate documents, getting them sent by special delivery because there's a postal strike. Make appointments with building society managers and close bank accounts. They all add up to make everyday life a huge mountain to climb. I feel as though I'm pushing boulders up hills all the time. I hate having to think about the need to sort things out. I need to put his photos in an album, but I can't do it. I can't sort through that series of images where he is so full of life, because I know the future and I can't stop it, I know where all these photos lead.

I hate it that I think about him slowly rotting in his coffin. How do I stop these thoughts? I think about the way he died, and hope he didn't suffer. I hope he knew absolutely nothing about his death – that it just felt like a shove rather than actually feeling any pain. I hate the fact that other people can get on with their lives, when ours are now disjointed and painful.

I know that there was life before Cyrus and that there will be life after him, I just have to get to that place – but the glue makes it such a very long, hard journey. I also know that I will never be one hundred per cent happy again, or feel one hundred per cent whole. That is something that truly saddens me. I hope the boys will be able move forward and perhaps, with good fortune and a little bit of luck, reach ninety-nine per cent. They will always have Cyrus in their hearts, but I hope he will allow them to go on and make great lives for themselves. I will wear my coat of sadness always, though I know that over time it will be visible only to me.

September already, and its Zac's birthday today; he's twenty-two. Where on earth did those years go? He was struggling last week, perhaps it was the lead-up to today, and the fact that Cyrus can't participate any more, and won't be having any more birthdays himself – well not ones that he will know about. Zac too, has bad days, worse days and occasionally unbearable days. Perhaps those are triggered by anniversaries, but sometimes a mere thought or memory can result in an unbearable day.

Thankfully not many people know what it feels like to have lost a sibling or a child so they can't understand how we feel about things like birthdays. Christmas is going to be impossible. I can't even begin to think how we will get through the day sober. I know I won't be sending any Christmas cards this year – who knows, maybe I'll never send one ever again. What would I write and from whom would I send it? I can't even begin to think down that road yet.

I'm perfectly aware of the fact that life goes on. I watch people walking down the street, sitting in cafés drinking coffee, pushing prams, breathing and laughing. I simply don't feel part of it any more. I wish I could paint over it all, and start again each morning.

I'm also acutely aware of how my mood affects the boys. I don't want to bring them down when they've managed to pull themselves out of their holes. I've said it before – I don't want them to think that Cyrus is the only person I ever think of. Yes, he was the middle one and was more demanding; needed more attention, constantly needing to know he was the best, loved the most, was the favourite son – not that he was, though – there were no favourites. I hope the boys know this, even with his death. Competitive to a fault, if there was any competition he would want to win. To be the first to the summit of a rocky outcrop on a beach in Wales, he would push Steely to the floor, even though he was far quicker and more athletic. Even knowing he would get a scolding from Rob, the fact that he had got there first far outweighed any consequences. He had won. That was Cyrus.

I'm sad for the fact that they won't ever have the chance to talk to him again – to share a cigarette, a Sambuca or a game of Pro. I hate it, and there's nothing I can do. My powers have gone, my ability to nurture has been erased. It must surely come back in time – but not now.

If you lose an eye or a leg, I suppose it must take time to readjust to your new perspective. You have to rebalance. I guess that's where I'm at. I have to learn to rebalance my life, and yet I wonder if those who lose limbs ever subconsciously realise that they have gone. I've heard that amputees still feel pain or an itch in their missing limb, and perhaps that is what I feel, having lost a child. I know he's gone, but the itching pain is still there.

Still September, and Steely is eighteen today. He said with tears in his eyes that Cyrus had promised to come home, and take him to the pub. What the hell do I say to that? I can't help him with the things that were promised and now will never be done. I can't make this better, and

I feel useless – not a proper mother any more. Where is my ability to heal? Only time will help with the pain, but the ability to heal has left now. I'm sorry, Steely my darling, he can't keep that promise. I hope you will forgive him for not being here to share that first legal drink, to hear you play your drums, to watch you grow into the man I know you've become.

Ever since June and the day we were handed Cyrus's dog-tags, Steely has desperately wanted a tattoo; now he's eighteen, he can have it. He knows exactly whom he wants to do it – Lal Hardy of New Wave Tattoos in Muswell Hill. He tattoos footballers; he comes highly recommended – only he will do. A tattoo would be symbol of his love, a symbol of who Cyrus was, a permanent reminder of what he has lost. He now proudly carries the tattoo of those dog-tags, Army number and chain as though they were physically wrapped around his forearm.

I wonder about tattoos. What is it about them that makes people want them? I know too that there are many who dislike them, or have had them done and regretted it later. I have one of a Celtic knot in the shape of a heart with Cyrus's name above it on the nape of my neck, even though I can't see it I know it's there – his name carved permanently into my skin, as it is etched into my brain, a constant reminder of a son lost, but never forgotten.

I know that Zac too will have one done – but not yet. He needs to work through it, design it – make it much more personal, so as to not be just another tattoo on his already tattooed body. Rob has tattoos too, but they are the random images from a youth long gone. He will not have one for Cyrus – not because he doesn't think he is worth it, but more because he would feel it disrespectful to place something so meaningful alongside his eclectic collection of Indian ink.

Many of Cyrus's friends have had commemorative tattoos since – his Army number, the date of his death – some large and obvious, but most small, secret, discreet. Several of his comrades from 10 Platoon have had them done too. Craig Monahan (Moni) has a scroll covering his back with these words: *We few, we happy few, we band of brothers, for who sheds his blood with me, will forever be my brother! RIP fallen brothers of 2009.* Elliott has Cyrus's initials and date of death on the inside of his wrist – always there where he can see it – his constant reminder, not that he needs a tattoo for that.

These tattoos have such a deep meaning because they were there, they fought side by side, and they will carry those memories with them always. Perhaps this is the only way they can externalise those memories, and remind others of the fact that they were actually there, and that all of these men must never be forgotten.

Certainly these tattoos are immensely personal, but I sometimes wonder why some people have had them done. Is it for their own benefit, a mark of respect, or so that they can absorb some of the attention that has been lavished on those these tattoos represent?

Steely has a gig tonight. It will be nice to go and watch him play – it is good for all of us, giving us a moment of freedom. I hope so much that his dreams come true, and his ambition of going to college in Los Angeles comes to fruition. He deserves it. I love watching him perform; he seems to go into a zone I can't reach, and it makes me so proud. It is lovely to see him relax and leave the anguish to one side for a few hours – smile at Zac and laugh with his friends. I want to stand up and shout that he's our son, look how good he is. Sad, I know, but that's what my children make me want to do. I want people to look at them and see them as I do.

I wonder if my friends look at me and think, 'I told you so'. I would always say, when they asked if I was worried about Cyrus going to Afghanistan, that he was more likely to be killed in this country by a drunk driver, or stabbed in a post-club brawl. I suppose that I used the statistics as a way of coping. But truthfully I <u>didn't</u> worry about him going to war. He was well trained, surrounded by people who were equally well trained, and who were there to look out for each other. The forces have a job to do, and they do it to the best of their ability – and then some. I did, however, worry every time he came home on leave and went into town. Squaddies are not popular, although quite why I'm not sure. Perhaps it is their fearlessness or arrogance.

I think that perhaps my rationale was that, had a drunk driver killed him, his death would have been pointless. Some would say that his death has been pointless, but then if we don't have an army we lay ourselves open to all the evil in the world, and our freedom within the Western World would be overthrown. I think that people forget why we fight tyranny. I personally find it irritating that I can't take a lipstick or bottle of water on to an aeroplane these days. I don't think the average person in this country equates that to terrorism and dominance. I don't want to live in a country where I can't travel freely, or be oppressed by a regime that doesn't allow women to work or have a voice. That is what Cyrus was fighting for – our liberty.

These men and women take on the role of protector, and we mustn't forget that. They chose their paths in life; no one, at any stage, has dragged them from their comfy beds, stuck a gun in their hand and told them to go to war. Those days have gone. They elect to do this job, and they all fully understand the consequences. Perhaps they are metaphorically our kamikaze pilots.

Cyrus said to me before he left that to die 'Killed in Action' was the highest honour, and the only way he would want to die. Who am I to deny him that? He was a man, making adult decisions and he didn't need the pressure of knowing that I would worry and disagree with his choices – which I didn't. He, along with the other fallen men and women, will go down in history as heroes, and hopefully the saviours of the free world. They will always be remembered each year by those who never met them, but who appreciate the job they did, and the sacrifices they have made. It doesn't make it any easier for us as a family, but it makes us even prouder. I just wish that it would help take the pain away.

CHAPTER 10

MEDALS PARADE

I wonder how the other twelve bereaved families are doing. We all have a common thread and yet I think that meeting them in Northern Ireland is going to be very hard. We each go with our own grief, and yet it is a shared grief. We have all lost, and yet our loss is too personal to share. It will be strange. I'm very nervous about it but I know it is something that has to be done; it too is part of the healing process. We need to talk to those soldiers and tell them how very proud we are of them, and that we think of them every day, and hope that they are physically and mentally strong enough to carry on.

I suppose some of them will come to the end of their obligatory four years soon, and I wonder how many of them from C Company will stay in the Army after this tour is over. I would like to think that Cyrus would have stayed on. He was Army material; when he signed up his intention was to serve his twenty-two years, get his full pension and still be only forty when he came out. He would never have settled in civvie life – I think it would have been too mundane, and after the horror of war he would have needed to be with people who were also there and understood the nightmares. Who knows?

I still have nightmares – but theirs are real. Mine are only in my imagination; theirs are fact. I worry about how they will cope when they get back after losing friends, seeing others mangled and maimed. How does the human mind cope with this? I know that there are many people who step up and help, giving them space to shout and scream, listen to them, soothe them with words and actions. I also know that there are people who would help me, but part of me resists their help. How do they truly know what I'm going through or how those boys will feel when they get back to 'normal' life? If they've not experienced it all first-hand, how do they know what will help? I'm not sure that my grief is covered in any textbook, nor the grief of anyone else. I don't think that I fall into the category of a 'standard' grieving parent. Who set the standard anyway?

We went to Ireland on Wednesday 4th November, 2009 to the Homecoming and Medals Parade. Our neighbour dropped us off at Heathrow, just as we had done for Cyrus so many times. I could feel my body start to constrict as we drew closer. So many memories, so many hugs so many waves goodbye. I wish I had never had to say goodbye.

Ian met us there and we were taken into the upgrade lounge. Free crisps, papers and drinks; the boys were amused by it, as we never normally get anything free when we travel anywhere.

There were other parents there too. Parents who, like us, were lost and parents whose boys had been injured.

All wondering what the next few days would bring, all not quite able to make eye contact.

It was such a hard journey to make, and I felt sick on the plane knowing that he had made this trip many times before – and not all that long ago. He hated flying, said he didn't like the shape of aeroplanes, that it didn't feel natural to be sitting in a metal tube jetting though the air.

We were met at Belfast City Airport by an army driver in a bus. The only other people I recognised were Jonathan, Margaret, Hannah and Jack Mervis. Driving through the lanes and past the places that Cyrus had also driven past was so painful. How could a house or a tree that I'd never set eyes on before make me feel so bloody awful?

It was dark when we arrived on base and Elliott was there to meet us, shivering in the cold. Slim and long-limbed with mousy hair so short it's hard to determine its colour properly, eyes drained of colour – perhaps they're blue or perhaps they're brown. Eyes that have seen too much.

We gave him a hug but I wish it could have been Cyrus. I can only imagine what strength it took to stand there, waiting for the family of his dead best friend. What thoughts of self-doubt crossed his mind? Should he have saved him? Could he have saved him? Could he have changed something that day so that it never happened? Is he as numb as us? I fear he is and that it will take him his whole lifetime to come to terms with his loss. They had a friendship that only a few lucky people manage to achieve. I so wish he didn't have to go through this pain. I wish I could absorb it all, take it into my body, and save all those who loved him from the agony his loss has left.

We all appeared quite calm – still in shock. I wonder if we reacted as he expected. Should we have been different, or was it as Cyrus would say, 'Man the fuck up,' whenever things got tough. Was Elliott expecting a grief-stricken family? The anaesthetic effect of this whole overwhelming process was protecting both him and us. Was he wondering if we would put the pressure of blame on his already straining shoulders? No, we would never have done that. Cyrus just stepped off the road at the wrong time. Elliott will always have a special place in my heart and I must remember to tell him one day.

They showed us to the house where we would be staying for the next thirty-six hours, a house on the base that would have normally accommodated a military family. They gave us half an hour to get ourselves sorted before going to the Serjeant's Mess for drinks and something to eat. It was dark and cold as we walked across the barracks to the mess. It just felt wrong. We were here for the wrong reasons; Cyrus should have been there to meet us.

I think we were given a brief outline of what would happen the next day. It was going to be busy – not much time to think too hard about the whole process, just get from 'a' to 'b' quickly and efficiently, get everything done on time without any hiccups – typical British Army. All we really wanted to do was find Elliott and go and meet the other soldiers.

As we were leaving the mess we asked about Leon Smith. We'd not seen him and wondered if he was on the base. Apparently he had been confined to quarters as it was suspected he had caught swine flu. I couldn't believe we wouldn't have the chance to meet up with him. Then we were whisked secretly into an accommodation block, where we knocked on a door.

The last time we had seen Leon was at Paul Mervis's funeral, where he had looked haggard, full of self-blame and sadness. It is such a pity that we never had the opportunity to meet him under different circumstances, when both Cyrus and Paul were alive.

Momentarily there was a flash of shock across his handsome face, but it was instantly replaced by a welcoming smile. He must have known we were attending The Homecoming, and that he had to represent both the Platoon and Paul, but I'm sure he wasn't expecting to see us at his door that evening. We had perhaps unfairly taken him by surprise. There must have been a part of him that dreaded this day, meeting us again. I wonder if things would possibly have been easier if we'd been the sort of people who had blame, and couldn't face him.

His white teeth shone against the contrast of his somewhat Mediterranean complexion – dark hair, even darker eyes – and there remained a slight scar on his chin, a physical reminder of that terrible day in Helmand Province. His is not a very tall man – under six foot – but he is powerfully built, thanks to hours of drills and workouts, I guess. His embrace was warm, and I said I didn't think he looked particularly ill. He replied that he felt fine, but wasn't allowed out of his quarters until he'd been seen by a doctor in the morning. He was clearly frustrated by what must have felt like such a seemingly insignificant suspected illness, stuck inside unable to be part of his and Paul's Platoon's Homecoming – but orders are orders. We left after a few minutes with the promise that he would, by hook or by crook, seek us out the next day so we could talk properly. It was good to see him. I so wish Cyrus could have been there.

We went with Elliott to the Rifleman's bar and met some of the soldiers; exhausted men with glazed eyes, trying to come to terms with the fact they were home. At first they didn't know where to look, how to approach us, what they should talk about. These young men who had come back from war, having faced unimaginable situations head on, looked uncertain in our company – their training hadn't included this. They are here, he is not. They were gutted for us, gutted for themselves – unable to express how they felt. We all made a huge effort to keep it together, but the whole evening bordered on breakdown by everyone – I wonder, though, if that might have been a good thing.

We knew they were looking at us thinking, wondering – do we blame, do we hate? Should they justify? There is no justification needed – we don't hate, can't blame. They didn't justify, they didn't have to explain – to do so would have been disrespectful. Theirs is a shared sorrow, he was their brother, Zac and Steely's brother, our son – their loss is our loss. I thought of the words I'd heard so many times from Cyrus, 'Man the fuck up,' so between us, we did. Names we'd heard we could now put faces to: Vaughny, Marshy, Tommo, Fun-Time, Stracs and Youngie.

Slowly we all relaxed and they started to talk to us about Cyrus, recounting stories of times they dressed up as women and went out on the town; Cyrus wearing impossibly tiny fuchsia-pink hot-pants and a glittery boob-tube; the pre-Afghanistan party where they had all dressed as cow-boys sporting false handle-bar moustaches. The laughter that radiated out of him everywhere he went, the ribbings he gave them. Marshy told us of the time Cyrus took the laces out of his trainers, cut out the zip of his jeans and removed all the buttons from his shirt, leaving him with nothing to wear on a weekend trip away. The angrier Marshy got, the louder they all laughed. Of all of them it is Marshy who looks, and possibly is, the youngest. He is tall and slim with mousey blonde hair and has a gentle Devonshire accent. They all seem tall, these boys – perhaps because I'm only five foot four everyone seems to tower above me.

They admired Cyrus's wiry strength as he was a light machine-gunner – it's not a thing I'd want to carry too far, weighing 8.5 kgs with 100 rounds, a 5.56-calibre weapon also known as a SAW – a squad automatic weapon. It's a gun designed to be employed by an individual soldier with or without assistance – an infantry support weapon used to fire short bursts. Tommo is a light machine-gunner and he is well over six foot tall, wide-chested, square-chinned – I guess it's a testament to Cyrus's tenacity and stamina that he was one too.

They all agreed that Paul Mervis's tribute couldn't have said it better:*'The darker and colder the night, the bigger was his smile. The hotter and longer the day, the louder was his laugh.'* It seemed that that was what they were all going to miss most – his sense of humour, his laugh and his huge smile. He seemed so alive when they talked of him, his antics still made them laugh – but there was emptiness in that laughter.

Rob thanked them for the flowers they had asked to be sent to Cyrus's funeral – a large floral tribute with the number 10 and the word 'Platoon' in green and red chrysanthemums. Apparently, when Leon Smith went back out to Afghanistan, he had talked about the funeral, saying one of the things he remembered most was all the beautiful young women, dressed in black, looking stunningly glamorous but totally devastated. He said that it was rather like being at a photo-shoot for *OK* or *Hello Magazine*. It was true, and Cyrus would have loved it.

The uncertainty of how the family of a fallen comrade will react must be so hard. I guess that some families will never be able to look those men in the eye without feeling some sort of resentment. I have no resentment – just sorrow. I know that any one of them could have been killed – it is just the 'luck of the draw', as Cyrus used to say. 'If your time is up, then it's up, and there's not a lot you can do about it – you just have to believe that you're going to be one of the lucky ones,' he had said before he left. I wish he had been one of the lucky ones. I wish we weren't here talking to these men, who have seen such awful things, who were such a huge part of his life, and who found it in themselves to carry on the fight. I so wanted him to be here, laughing and joking with them, not just a memory.

A tall, blonde man approached on crutches. His three-quarter-length trousers revealed his prosthetic leg. I didn't recognise him at first – the last time I had seen him he was in a wheelchair. It was Willo (Matt Wilson).

I was surprised that he was so tall; the last time we met he was so hunched – and now he had regained weight. He looked good, but tired. He gave us a hug, it was good to see him. I wish Cyrus was with us.

They kicked us out eventually, together with the rest of the Riflemen who had eked out their last drinks. Several rounds of Sambuca were bought – strange how so many of them grimaced as they downed their shots. I assumed that they would all have liked the drink. It was Cyrus's favourite and I'm sure it will always remind them of him. He used to make Steely drink it, so he could laugh at his face as it burned its way down his throat. Many a hangover was caused by Sambuca.

The next morning, after breakfast, Ian met us and took us across to the Officer's Mess where we were going to be presented with The Elizabeth Cross by Viscount Brookeborough of Colebrooke, County Fermanagh. Tea and biscuits, in china cups with saucers, and nowhere to put them down as everything is antique and I didn't want to mark the surfaces. Ridiculous. Fancy worrying about making a mark on some furniture when we are just about to meet the Viscount.

The Elizabeth Cross is traditionally presented to the next of kin and that person is determined by rules far older than I. The father is first in line, so it was Rob who was presented with the Cross, otherwise it would be the mother then any siblings in order of age, unless the soldier had a child, in which case they are next of kin, followed by the spouse then the parents and siblings. Quite complicated and I can understand why there is so much confusion when marriages have split, and parents are not sure who is actually next of kin, rather than just assuming they are because they always have been on any forms that have been filled out in the past. I had always put myself as next of kin simply because I was the one who was around at home more, and I suppose usually I'd filled in the forms. Rob accepted the Cross on behalf of us all as a family.

There were two Crosses in the box – one large, for formal attire, and one smaller for everyday wear, if you were the sort of person who wore a suit to work. I know what I'd rather have pinned to my lapel – but that is never to be. Is it an honour? I'm not sure. A piece of silver doesn't make it all better and it's not the sort of thing that Rob or I would wear everyday – and even if one did, only those in the know would actually understand its significance. Something else to put in the chest underneath his photos in the front room.

Again, it's all wrong. He should be here receiving his operational medal, not us receiving the Elizabeth Cross. I don't want silver – I want him.

At 11 o'clock, inside a huge canvas building that looked rather like an aircraft hangar, the Memorial Service was held. The whole battalion plus all their families, dignitaries and the bereaved were there. We, the bereaved and injured, had seats towards the front; everyone else stood. It was crowded, and searching through the faces I strained to see ones I recognised, but there were none. There was a strong wind blowing and the gusts crossing the top of the canvas roof made a sound like running feet. I wonder if I was the only one to think this was strange and perhaps a little unnerving. I don't believe in ghosts but it certainly sounded as though people were running across the roof.

2 Rifles lost thirteen during their six-month deployment as part of 19 Light Brigade in Afghanistan:

Rifleman Adrian Sheldon, 25 – 7th May 2009
Rifleman Cyrus Thatcher, 19 – 2nd June 2009
Lieutenant Paul Mervis, 27 – 12th June 2009
Corporal Johathan Horne, 28 – 10th July 2009
Rifleman Daniel Simpson, 20 – 10th July 2009
Rifleman Joseph Murphy, 18 – 10th July 2009
Rifleman William Aldridge, 18 – 10th July 2009
Rifleman James Backhouse, 18 – 10th July 2009
Rifleman Aminiasi Toge, 26 – 16th July 2009
Captain Mark Hale, 42 – 13th August 2009
Rifleman Daniel Wilde, 19 – 13th August 2009
Serjeant Paul McAleese, 29 – 20th August 2009
Acting Serjeant Stuart McGrath, 28 – 16th September 2009

Thirteen families, mourning the loss of their precious sons. Some had come from so far away – there are a lot of Fijians in the British Army and they too were there to pray for the souls of those lost. Halfway through the service there was a lot of shuffling of boots and then several Fijian men and a couple of women moved to the front and started to sing a traditional Fijian lament. It sent shivers up and down my spine – no music just small bits of paper to read from and the most amazing harmony of voices soaring up to the ceiling, filling the whole place with the sound of their pride, pain and love. They really are massive, these Fijian men and there was not a dry eye amongst them, or the congregation. So beautiful, so sad, so poignant – such feeling in those words. More tears on another sad day to add to our collection.

Elliott met us outside. He wanted to introduce us to his family, their joy at his safe return marred by the loss of their son's best friend. I wished we were that family, there to see their boy home and safe. Their pain for us was obvious, but I was determined to let them know that I was pleased at their son's safe return.

More food, tea and coffee before the Medals Parade, so time to gather ourselves and focus on the next stage of the day. It is a huge base and we seemed to spend an awful lot of time walking from one side of it to the other. I wonder if this is partly to keep us moving and therefore not thinking too much, or it's just the size of the battalion that I'd not really thought about before, but we were on automatic pilot anyway.

It's very cold in Northern Ireland, especially in November, when the wind cuts across the fields running down from the Mourne Mountains. I don't think I was warm at any stage during our visit. We reached the parade field and there were marquees for the families, which offered some protection from the wind.

Over five hundred men and women stood to attention on that field. The wind cut across them but no-one moved; they waited while Field Marshal The Lord Edwin Bramell stood on the dais and spoke with a voice that did not tremble or fall, piercing the wind, telling them how proud he was of them, what a sacrifice they as a battalion had made, and that they should hold their heads high and be proud of what they had achieved for the Afghan people and for the peoples of the free world. His words echoed around the parade field – words of pride and glory. He spoke with eloquence and beauty, and all were moved. There was no other sound apart from the wind rippling against the marquees. It wasn't just his age and rank that captivated everyone; his words were perfect and encompassed every emotion there that day.

All the injured were given their medals first, presented by the Field Marshal who is one of the last Field Marshals alive, as there is no such rank any more, and Lieutenant General Sir Nick Parker, Colonel Commandant of 2 Rifles and Deputy Commander of ISAF, whom we'd met at Lyneham only a few months ago.

They stood there, solid and proud, those soldiers, while the wind brought horizontal rain to whip their legs and faces, and the dignitaries moved among them, shaking their hands and talking quietly to each and every one. Not until the last medal had been presented and the 'quick march' order was given did they move, and then as one they turned to face their families, saluted and quick marched off the field. Together Rob and I held hands and cried. He wasn't there saluting proudly to the crowd. How is it that he is not there? Oh God, it's just too sad to bear. I didn't think I had anything left to break, but we stood there and broke all over again into thousands of pieces. Perhaps it is true – he is not coming home.

Later we were taken to the Community Centre and served more tea. By now Steely decided that if he were to see another cup of tea again he would scream. Still, you couldn't say that we were not extremely well looked after by everyone we met. Elliott, Malou, Marsh and several others were there too. I'm not sure if they asked to be present or if they just decided to turn up, but it was nice to see familiar faces. We'd briefly met Malou the evening before; he was one of the soldiers who hadn't been receiving food parcels and Cyrus had asked us if we could send him some bits and pieces, as it upset him that Malou didn't get anything addressed specifically to him. We continued to send Malou parcels, even after Cyrus was killed and until they came home in September. It was the least we could do, and in every parcel Rob wrote him a note. He told Rob he had kept every one of those notes, and that he would always keep them as they meant so much to him. That was nice – but again, edged with such sadness.

Malou's eulogy to Cyrus read:

> *"I don't know where to start or what to say, but what I know is that we will miss you a lot. We will never forget you – we will always remember you. You were more than just a friend in the Platoon. You were always there when people felt down; you cared about people. You never wanted any return on the kindness you and your family provided.*
>
> *When I wasn't receiving any parcels, your parents sent me some to keep me going. For that I thank you.*
>
> *May your soul rest in peace; may God be with you. We will always love and remember you for who you really are. Mate, when we meet again, the fun will really begin. Goodbye, Thatch mate, it was an honour to know you."*

Then the Field Marshal was ushered in and he presented us with a silver bugle. He was such a nice old man, who had fought in several wars and was genuinely sorry for our loss – sorry for so many losses in the past. He is well practised in this sorrow. No consolation though, this silverware – just another reminder of what we've lost, something else to put on a shelf and have to polish and dust. I know I sound ungrateful, but I'm not. It's just not what I want; more reminders of what I don't have any more.

As we stood talking to some of the soldiers, Ali Gordon (G) came in and introduced himself as one of Cyrus's friends from 10 Platoon. They had become good friends and Cyrus and Elliott had spent a lot of time with him and his young family. It is very odd meeting people that you've heard so much about under these circumstances, as no one is quite sure how to approach us or what to say when they do. He asked if he could bring his family in to meet us, his wife Liza, youngest daughter Lucy and Morgan, his eight-year-old daughter, who had something for us. She had bought a box of Hero chocolates that she was going to give Cyrus when he came back, but instead she spent all night making us a card for him.

She was so sad, this little girl with her long blonde hair, wearing a woollen hat and winter coat, and there was nothing I could do to help. I wished there was. She was so completely devastated by his death – they had been great friends. How could we explain this to her? How can this little girl be so sad? There was nothing I can do to help. It was so awful to see her little face distorted with pain and disbelief. I guess I'd not really thought how much his death would affect those people he touched in his short time here in Ireland. All she could say was that he'd promised to come home and marry her. Oh God, Morgan, I don't know what to say to you. I don't know – I'm so sorry, my sweet.

I promised that I'd send her a photo of him, as the only one she has she cut out of the newspaper. She is only eight, with so much pain and sadness now resting on her little shoulders. 'He'd promised to come home,' was all she could say through her tears, and I didn't know how I was supposed to answer. How on earth could I help her through? In my own selfish way I guess I thought that only we could feel this much pain, but looking at her little face so sad and confused, I knew then that I was wrong. He was so good with children – well, anyone he met – and made them feel special and that they were the only person in the world. How could we have lost that?

When we got back we sent her a photo in a silver frame. I hope she liked it. I hope that in due course she will be able to look back fondly at the time she knew him, keep all the nice things in her heart and move away from the horror of loss – that she keeps his memory close, hearing him laugh as she looks at that smile. I hope for her, I hope for me, I hope for Rob and the boys.

That evening, back on the parade field, there were fireworks and the battalion band. Stirring stuff, all those bugles, bagpipes and drums. I think the sound of a bugle will always make the hairs stand up on my neck. Pride and pain in a clear pure note.

Later that evening, after we'd been thrown out of the Rifleman's Bar at closing time, we were heading back to the house when Leon Smith asked if we'd like one more drink in the Serjeant's Mess. Why not, who knows when we'll next see him? It was quiet in the mess but the bar was still open, so with closing time looming, Leon went off to get enough drinks for us all to last a while.

It was good for us all to have the chance to talk to him. I think he needed to get things off his chest too. He talked with fondness of Cyrus, both as a soldier and a man. He reiterated what we had heard in the Rifleman's Bar. He talked about Cyrus's fitness – that he was fast, agile, strong, fazed by nothing, completely reliable. His dedication was total – no order was too hard, no command ever questioned, and he was thoughtful and compassionate. He was a complete soldier, including his ability to keep morale high – which was part of the reason Leon had picked him as part of his Quick Reaction Force. This is perhaps partly responsible for his feelings of guilt. He had chosen him that day; perhaps that's why he said at Paul's funeral that he would never forgive himself.

Listening to him talk, I was filled with pride. I'd read the tributes, heard the stories, seen the love for him in these soldiers' eyes; but the truth is that it should be him here, sharing their tales of war and comradeship, and collecting medals – not us, his broken and devastated family.

Steely was very quiet, and when Leon went off to the bar he took the opportunity to follow him. They were gone a long time but when they returned, Steely seemed slightly easier. It wasn't until much later that I learnt that he had asked Leon what had happened in Afghanistan. He didn't want to know the gory details, just the events leading up to the explosion. I think it helped him, as he seemed to accept it for what it was, and move forward a little. He needed to hear it from Leon, and I'm glad he did. I know that Zac would never have been able to ask those questions out loud. He has shut down, I can't reach him, and he deals with his pain in his own way by locking himself away. It makes me feel useless and I hope one day he will feel able to talk to me – allow me in. I don't know if he and Steely ever discussed what was said, and I often wonder where Steely stores these secrets and if they will raise their ugly heads one day. I know he hurts as much as everybody else, but he appears to be level-headed, and is able to use the tools Cyrus left in his letter, take those words and make them into something positive. It must be very hard for them to live in the footsteps of their brother, but I know over time this will change. They will start making their own imprints, living their lives as their own people again. I hope there won't be any resentment mixed in with their sorrow.

Leon was wearing a Rifles' Regimental tie that is dark green with black diagonal stripes outlined in red. Zac asked where he could get one – if he could get one – as he'd like one as a memento. Leon immediately took it off and gave it to him. Rob said that he liked the look of his trousers, Leon gave a wry smile – enough said. It lightened the atmosphere, and helped us all relax a little.

It was after 3 am when we eventually said goodbye to Leon. Back in our house, exhausted by the day and knowing we had to be up in four hours, we were almost too tired to sleep. Cyrus had been based in Northern Ireland for eighteen months and will never come back. I've been here for thirty-six hours – and I'll not come back. There is nothing here for me in Ballykinler.

CHAPTER 11

REMEMBRANCE DAYS

I dreamt of him again the other night, with such a feeling of reality it left me breathless. We were in Caversham, waiting for the Remembrance Day Parade to come along so we could join it. There was a little girl with pigtails, sitting on a bench opposite me, drawing. Rob was looking out into the street. Then there he was, walking around the corner with a black leather trenchcoat on, his hands in his pockets. 'Hello Mum,' he said in a low, solemn voice. 'I can't hear you very well,' he said as he leant against me for a hug. I stroked his hair – I could feel his hair! He was pale and I knew he was dead but I could feel the weight of him and the texture of his hair. 'I'm ok now, I'm playing Pro,' he whispered. 'I just can't hear you very well because of my ears.' I looked at Rob and he spoke to the little girl who obviously couldn't see Cyrus and was wondering why I was crying and stroking thin air. Rob could see him and when he explained to the girl that it was Cyrus, she shrugged her little shoulders and carried on with her drawing. I woke crying. I had felt the pressure of his body on mine – how could this be? I know he is ok – it's the rest of us who aren't.

Are these dreams messages, or is it my imagination trying to help me cope with the enormity of what has happened? That's twice now that he's spoken, and both times to say he's ok.

Sometimes I wished I believed in a God and heaven – it would make it easier to think that he was somewhere, playing Pro or listening to music, watching and waiting. I wish, but I don't, and even this tragedy won't change my feelings on gods and such. I'm glad, though, that other people get comfort from their beliefs. So many have written, 'Until we meet again' or, 'When we meet again.' I can see why religion is appealing to some – just not to me. I would ask too many questions like, 'Why my child?' and expect the answers that I wanted to hear. But then I suppose that the answer would be that it is not for us to choose who lives or dies, but we have to accept that it's for a reason, whatever that reason might be.

That would not be of any comfort to me. I still want him back. Sitting in the bath, I wonder what I've done to deserve this. Why should I have to go and tend a garden on a grave? Why should I have to go out and see his friends carrying on with their lives? Why should this have happened to us? All these questions make my throat dry and my eyes sore, but I ask them all the same. Sobs rack my body and the pain seems insurmountable. Too many questions that will never be answered; after all, who has an answer and anyway, who would I ask them of?

An invitation had come through the post for us to go The Royal Albert Hall on Saturday for the Festival of Remembrance. There seems to be such a lot going on this week. I suppose I'd not really thought about Remembrance Sunday and all that goes with it. Over the years I've watched it on the telly, but then I wasn't part of that life. I am now.

Another reason to panic about what to wear, the Queen will be there – not that she'll see me but still, I need something to wear. I hate it, I hate shopping, I hate the fact that I have to choose something that is out of my comfort zone. I would do it a thousand times though for him. I just wish I didn't have to.

Dianne, Sharpie's mum, has kindly said she would drive us up to London and wait while we went in and took part in the Festival. People can be so very kind. It's strange how those you thought would step up to the mark don't, and those who do come unexpectedly out of the blue.

Another unexpected thing happened. The phone rang at 8.50 on Friday morning, and it was BBC Radio Berkshire's Breakfast Programme to say that they had some good news about Cyrus and Remembrance Day, and would I stay on the line so they could tell me 'live' on the radio? I texted Rob and told him what was going to happen so he could switch the radio on at work. I couldn't think what it could be – what possible good news? To be honest, there can't be any. Still, I waited until they were ready then Andrew Peach, the presenter, informed me (and anyone else listening) that the Caversham Branch of the Royal British Legion had decided that Cyrus's name should be engraved on the

War Memorial down by the Thames in Caversham. No name had been added since World War II and there was a panel that had been left blank with the hope that it would never have another name added to it. They felt it was the least they could do, this honour for our son. It is overwhelming, it truly is. He had touched the hearts of so many people that he'd never met. An honour and yet…

I was then called by The Legion and we were invited to join them on Sunday morning at 11 am. Steel yourself for more tears and pain, Helena.

The Royal Albert Hall is a very beautiful building – I don't think I'd ever been inside before now. We got a drink before it all started and the curved corridors were lined with Legion Banners and men and women covered in medals. Once inside the Hall itself we were seated behind the band and the banner-bearers – all so very sad. Huge swathes of material hung from the ceiling and images were projected on to them.

Men from wars past spoke of their fallen comrades, and one that particularly affected me was a man in his late eighties or early nineties, with tears in his eyes and pain in his voice. He told of the day he was on the beaches of Northern France and his friend was shot, describing how he'd sat with him, held his hand, soothed him, and watched him die – powerless to do anything about it. Surrounded by gunfire, not considering that his own life was in danger, he had remained simply frozen, not wanting to leave his friend. He spoke as though it had happened yesterday. Tragic to think his loss still affects him after all these years – how much he still misses him, and how not a day has gone by without his friend being in his thoughts. It made me think of Elliott and wonder if one day he would be saying these things about Cyrus. It never stops, this pain, for me or anyone who has lost a friend and brother.

There were songs, marches and tributes from so many, both civilian and from the forces. Then the ceiling opened and thousands of tissue-paper poppy petals fell during the two-minute silence. They cascaded to the floor, a red curtain of paper petals landing on those below, who never moved a muscle. They are so proud, these men and women of our forces. Let us not forget.

Afterwards, people stooped and picked up handfuls of the petals, and the boys went down to the floor and collected some too. I have them safe inside the programme – more memories to add to my growing collection, and I wonder if I will ever look at it again.

There is no comfort in all these ceremonies – not for me anyway. It's just another emotionally draining day. Sunday morning was cold, typically, and we dressed warmly, knowing that we were going to stand outside for at least an hour down by the river. We'd already collected our wreath from the Legion and loading it and ourselves into the car we headed into Caversham.

So many people were heading towards the river. I'd never done this before so it took me by surprise. Then there were the faces of friends, shivering in the cold, sobbing into hankies, holding poppies and little wooden crosses. Rob's cousin Kieron came forward and gave us a handful of these crosses with the Rifles' emblem on them, I don't know where he got them, but it was a lovely gesture. There were Brownies, Scouts, elderly men covered in medals – and then I saw Elliott,

Marsh and a Serjeant from the Rifles, in their combats. We were surprised, we'd not known they were going to be there. The ceremony was quite quick and we were asked to come up while the last prayers were said. It was horrible, standing in front of all these people – some I knew, and some I didn't, my soul laid bare yet again to all the pain and anguish this awfulness brings. We laid our wreath, then the soldiers moved forward and laid theirs. This was the first time they'd been over from Ireland to see us since they got back from Afghanistan a few weeks earlier.

The press were there, and we spoke to several of them, but I was acutely aware that Elliott and Marsh were in the background, and I needed to get to them. There were friends we'd not seen for months, wanting to talk and tell us how sad they still were. There was a slight feeling of panic – we had to get up to the graveside. In addition we were going to London again in the afternoon as we'd been invited to an anti-war theatre production called 'Eloquent Protest'. Time was not on our side.

Zac hopped in the car with Elliott and Marsh and directed them to the cemetery. We were surprised to see how many people were already there. When Zac and the soldiers arrived I went and stood next to them. It was the first time that Elliott and Marsh had been at the graveside. It was all they could do to stand up straight. Here they were, looking at the grave of their best friend – the closest they'd been to him for months. We squeezed each other's hands, hugged and cried. 'This is such a shitty place to be,' I whispered. 'It's not fucking fair and not right that we are all standing here doing this.' Pain on top of pain for my boys, Rob, Elliott, Marsh, friends – we were all there for all the wrong bloody reasons. I didn't want anyone to have to stand in front of the grave of a nineteen-year-old – it was so wrong... and we had to rush – we needed to get to London. I felt awful about it when they had come specially to see us. Fuck. I knew they would be back, but it was really all too much.

So, another anniversary to add to the birthdays, Christmas, Remembrance Day, the date of his death – too many, too much, too bloody sad to even truly comprehend.

On this next trip Zac's friend Sharpie was our chauffeur. He drove us to Shaftsbury Avenue, where we had to be at The Duke of York's Theatre for the production of 'Eloquent Protest', at which the actor Jason Isaacs was going to be reading extracts from Cyrus's letters. Terri Judd, the journalist from 'The Independent' whom we had first met in Wootton Bassett, had arranged for us to meet Jason before the show. He explained that he'd been asked to recite some of Wilfred Owen's poetry, by the producers, but was so moved by Cyrus's letters, he asked to use them instead.

'They have the beauty and lyricism of a young boy of today, who could be walking past us in the street. Unlike the great poets of previous world wars, there is no ability to distance ourselves from it,' he said, when interviewed by 'The Independent'. 'His exhilaration at finally getting to do the thing he has lived and trained for and his attempt to communicate that to his family is very affecting. I am twice as old as Cyrus was, and I overthink and analyse. His words seem to come straight from the heart. There is no literary pretension. I felt like I was listening to a video diary rather than reading a letter.'

It was flattering that Jason wanted to share his interpretation of Cyrus's words, but because I knew nothing of 'Eloquent Protest', the whole thing was a completely new and bemusing experience. Sir Tony Benn was there as a speaker. There were people reciting poems – musicians, dancers and singers. They are all anti-war, but not in a fanatical way, but simply quietly and peacefully airing their views.

After the show we met Terri again to thank her, and say goodbye. She has been very kind and an enormous help with the press. I have telephoned her on several occasions since for advice – she is someone I trust and who has become a friend. Journalists sometimes get a bad press – admittedly deserved at times – however, we have been fortunate in our dealings with them, and have found them to be nothing but kind, sympathetic and professional, and we are grateful for that.

Sitting in the back of Sharpie's car on the clogged streets of London later that evening, we were completely exhausted. It had been a long and difficult weekend.

On Remembrance Day itself we went to Micklands Primary School, which all our three boys had attended. It seems such a long time ago that I walked along the main road to school with them all, running and laughing every day. We live only ten minutes from the school and it felt odd walking into the playground again, seeing all the small children with their bright red jumpers and grey skirts and trousers. They look so little – it's hard to imagine that my boys were ever that small.

At Micklands they have planted a memorial rose-garden and chose roses named Peace, Hero and Remember Me. They asked us to attend their assembly and help some of the children plant bulbs around the roses. It was a very sweet tribute and they had commissioned a brass plaque with Cyrus's name, stating that he had been a former pupil. It is still almost impossible for my brain to register seeing his name in stone or brass. I can't quite equate it to my life, although I know I have to come to terms with it.

It was here, at Micklands, that Cyrus met David May, who became his best friend – a friendship shared by both Zac and Steely, and which lasted through junior school, senior school and beyond. Whenever Cyrus was home on leave he would call David. Their personalities were so different, but their tastes and builds were similar; both were tall, slim and athletic, conscious of their looks – particularly about their hair. David's was fair, whereas Cyrus's was dark strawberry blonde. David would poke fun and call him 'ginger'. Both loved clothes, shoes and girls – but Cyrus was loud and fearless while David was shy and quiet. They shared a love of football, music and an identical sense of humour, and would spend long hours in the garage talking and laughing, listening to music and, as they got older, smoking and drinking, playing computer games. Pro was one of their favourites, but they also loved kicking a football around the garden. David became a huge part of our lives – he was included in family meals and holidays, and was never far away if Cyrus was around.

David is now the drummer in a band called The Kixx, and soon after Cyrus's death he wrote a song, which is now on their album. It is his tribute to a much loved and missed friend. The words reach out and are relevant to all friendships, but I know when I read the lyrics that it was written for Cyrus – and it's achingly sad.

Breathless

What happened to forever?
The promises we made,
The summers spent together,
Those silly games we played.
I guess promises get broken,
But not with you and me, yeah
You were everything I hoped –
I hoped that you would be, yeah.

So tell me what to do with all
The dreams that we had planned

I'm breathless.
I've never said how much I cared
And I'm sorry
That, my friend, I wasn't there.
I'm speechless – I'm falling – if I was there
I'd take the blow, oh no
Then you'd be coming home.

I wish I had the time
To say what I wanted to say –
To say how much you meant,
Before it all got taken away.
I waited here for days, for you

To come back now.
A taken heart so young –
Tell me, where's the sense in that, now?
So tell me what to do with all
The dreams that we had planned.

I'm breathless.
I never said how much I care,
And I'm sorry
That, my friend, I wasn't there.
I'm speechless. I'm falling – if I was there
I'd take the blow, oh no
Then you'd be coming home...
You'd still be coming home.

What happened to forever?
The promises we made,
The summers spent together,
Those silly games we played.

I'm breathless.
I've never said how much I care
And I'm sorry
That, my friend, I wasn't there.
I'm speechless. I'm falling – if I was there
I'd take the blow, oh no
Then you'd be coming home...
You'd still be coming home.

All these tributes, flowers and wreaths on the grave,
well-wishers, messages on Facebook, cards and letters,
texts and phone calls... It was a shame that there was

not so much as a brief call, or even a note in the post or a flower on the grave from Rob's dad, saying he was thinking of Cyrus and us. This was the outcome of a phone conversation six weeks earlier, when he had told me that he wouldn't talk about Cyrus as it hurt him too much to even say his name. I'd told him that he should be proud of Cyrus, and not pretend he didn't exist, but he is stubborn beyond belief, and I know it will be down to Rob to make contact, as he knows that his dad would rather never speak again than bow down and make amends.

From him there was no respect for Cyrus as a soldier or a grandson – no empathy shown to Rob, myself and the boys – and my mother was as guilty as Rob's dad. It was only when my sister Mione called, telling us that we had been in her thoughts, that I learned my mother was on holiday in Iran. No wonder there had been no contact. She wasn't even in the country. Iran? How disrespectful to Cyrus was it to be going on holiday, over the Remembrance period? How could she have continued with her holiday plans and go to this tyrannical country after what had happened? It had not occurred to either of them how hurtful we would find their behaviour.

Cyrus in Sangar 3, FOB Gibraltar, Afghanistan

Cyrus with me – whilst home on pre-tour leave March 2009

Cyrus, Zac and Steely – the last photo of our boys together March 2009, Reading

Steely, Cyrus, Rob and Zac with the crabs they caught off the Devon coast – summer 1997

Zac, Steely, Rob and Cyrus – Disneyland, Florida 1998

Steely, Rob, Cyrus and Zac – Mud baths in Turkey August 2002

Steely, me, Zac and Cyrus relaxing in the Jacuzzi after a day skiing in Fernie, British Columbia, Canada 2004

Rob, Cyrus and me – open day at ATR Bassingbourn – April 2007

"Chin Up, Head Down"

Namur Platoon, Marlborough Company ATR Bassingbourn 2007. Pte Cyrus Thatcher is top row, second from right.

Cyrus, Chief-of-Police, Lt. Paul Mervis – Kosovo 2008

Cyrus with children whilst protecting a monastery in Kosovo with Rfn Marsh in the background.

"Chin Up, Head Down"

Artwork by Lcpl Strachan, done to pass time whilst in the FOB, which stood outside the tented living area

10 Platoon, FOB Gibraltar, Afghanistan May 2009.
From left to right front row: Lcpl Strachan, Rfn Thompson, Lcpl
Wilson, Cpl Waldron, Cpl Childs, Lt Paul Mervis, Sjt Smith, Cpl
Kirkham, Lcpl Ells, Rfn Cyrus Thatcher, Rfn Vaughan. Back row: Rfn
Elliott (behind 50cal gun), Rfn Monaghan, Rfn Franks, Rfn Malou,
Rfn McGinn, Rfn Gordon, Rfn Reed, Rfn Young, Rfn Preist, Rfn Jacobs,
Rfn Hughes (behind 50cal gun)

"Chin Up, Head Down"

Cyrus and Rfn Stewart Elliott in their sleeping quarters, at Camp Bastion, Afghanistan

Paul Jacobs with Lasam the puppy in a patrol base outside FOB Gibraltar, Afghanistan

"Chin Up, Head Down"

Cyrus waiting to go out on patrol, FOB Gibraltar,
Afghanistan

Funeral of Cyrus at Reading Minister of St Mary the Virgin
Photo: Geoffrey Swaine / Rex Features

"Chin Up, Head Down"

Cyrus proudly wearing his Rifles beret

CHAPTER 12

SOLDIERS IN THE SNOW

On Wednesday we're off to the Dominican Republic for a week. We need to get away. We need some distraction. 'Go where no-one knows us or our story,' Zac said – and he's right. This whole process is intensely private – but intrusive too, as there seems no time or place to sit and try to assimilate all that has happened. Either we are soothing others or we are walking on broken glass around each other at home, afraid to say what we are really thinking and feeling, in case we hurt with our words. We move around each other, not truly being, just existing: this is no life for anyone. We really ought to try and talk, but it is too painful, too personal and too awful, so nobody knows what to say. Perhaps the sun will do us good. We've not been to the Dominican Republic before, so there are no memories – only new ones to make.

Huge empty blue skies, warm sea, a pool and endless cocktails – oh God, Cyrus would have loved it. This is not helping, it just emphasises the fact that he's not here with us any more. Strangely, the empty blue sky is almost the hardest thing to look at. His eyes were that blue; my heart is this empty, Zac and Steely are still lonely, Rob and I are now broken.

Getting away didn't help at all. We were just somewhere else – still feeling awful. There was no getting away from it – whom were we trying to kid? Perhaps it recharged our batteries a little, giving us a few days with moments when Cyrus was not constantly in the forefront of our thoughts – moments like the night we went to the sushi bar and Zac was asked to stand up and help the chef by chopping pieces of chicken and trying to flick them into the chef's hat that had been placed on his head.

Both Zac and Steely entered a table tennis competition, knowing they had no chance of winning because neither of them had played the game properly before. It was more a case of why not? Nothing to lose. The eventual winner gave them no end of laughs as he was so competitive and determined to beat everyone. With his large designer-stubbled jaw, they nicknamed him Chuck Norris.

They spent one morning in little James-Bond-style speedboats, bouncing out across the waves to a reef where they snorkelled and fed tropical fish. These were treasured moments when we could watch Zac and Steely leave the darkness of sorrow for an hour or so, smiling as they were somewhat distracted. It was lovely to see them smile – it seemed such a long time ago that they did; relaxed enough to allow themselves to breathe without pain.

Back in England, browner but not better – and we still couldn't talk about how we felt – it was still too soon.

I know they all have good and bad days, just like me – but I don't really know how they feel. I hate not being able to help them; my impotency returns to haunt me. It's only a couple of weeks now until Christmas, and I can't even start to think how to approach it or anticipate what new agonies it might bring. The tree, the decorations, the food, the presents, family... I don't know what to get for anyone – I don't want to go shopping, and I don't really care if Christmas comes or not. I don't really care about anything any more. I know that I have to go on because of the boys and Rob, but there truly are days when I just don't care. I have to drag myself out of bed in the mornings and paint on a fake smile. I hate talking to people who don't 'get it', but then how the hell <u>are</u> they supposed to 'get it' when they haven't experienced 'it'? What on earth am I thinking about? I've gone mad and the whole world just keeps on turning when I want to get off. I got stuck in a shop yesterday. I went into Caversham to buy some Christmas wrapping paper and I just got stuck. I couldn't find my money, I couldn't open my bag, I couldn't do anything but stand there and feel really stupid. I knew the lady in the shop as my boys and her children went to school together, but I just stood there and felt completely useless. We were both in tears. I left and phoned Debbie, my friend from my schooldays. Then I couldn't remember where I'd parked the car – for crying out loud, how fucking stupid have I become? I never lose control and there I was in a car park (the wrong one, mind you) looking for my car and panicking. I didn't even <u>need</u> wrapping paper – I've got a drawer full of it. I supppose I needed to do something positive about Christmas – but it was a disaster.

Zac, Cyrus and Steely always loved Christmas – I think it was their favourite time of the year. Rob and I loved it too – it was a time to be together and spoil our children – quality time. Rob and I would start planning for this day in October, and by the time Christmas Day arrived we would have so much food, and so many presents, that our excitement was equal to the boys'.

Every Christmas Eve we would get the boys to write their Christmas lists and send them up the chimney to Father Christmas. We would leave mince pies, carrots and milk out for him and his reindeer. Once the boys were in bed, stockings would be loaded, and the carrots, mince pies and milk made to look like they'd been feasted on.

We always woke before the boys, and would lie in bed waiting to hear them stir. They would sneak past our door, thinking we were asleep, and we'd listen as they tip-toed downstairs and fumbled around in the front room – one of them announcing, 'He's been! he's been!' The fact that Father Christmas had been seemed to be their cue, and waking Mum and Dad now didn't matter. They would stampede up the stairs and bounce on our bed. We would pretend they'd woken us, and Rob would insist that he, 'couldn't possibly get up without a cup of tea,' and, as this was Christmas Day, his favourite – a shortbread biscuit. They always accepted this but the tea was never finished before they would be pleading, 'Please, please, please can we go and open our stockings?' So downstairs we'd all go, and the next hour would be spent emptying their stockings of potato guns, yo-yos, tubs of plastic soldiers, bouncy balls, glasses with eyes on springs, socks and pants, their favourite sweets or chocolates – Zac's a box of Turkish Delight, Cyrus's Dime bars or Caramel bars and Steely's Haribo or Kinder Eggs. As they got older the stocking presents changed to deodorants, after-shave, CDs and Calvin Klein underpants – all opened with the same excitement.

Breakfast would start with Bucks Fizz, followed by a feast of kippers and kidneys, croissants and jam. Once we'd all had our fill, the table cleared, dishwasher loaded and the turkey put in the oven, we would retreat to the front room, where the next two hours would be spent opening our main presents. The boys enjoyed giving each other presents almost as much as receiving them.

Our best Christmases were the ones with just the five of us at home, with the door shut and the phone off the hook. One year Steely got a pair of Star Wars pyjamas and he stayed in them right up until New Year's Day. Visiting relatives always seemed to be hard work, and never relaxed – it would be awkward. Rob's dad would be uneasy, as he was out of his comfort zone, unable to relax and enjoy himself, and my mother thought the boys were over indulged and spoilt. It seems odd that she couldn't appreciate the fact that these little boys were simply having a lovely day – so what if they had lots of silly plastic things? We felt it was about us all being together, and sharing the joy they showed at getting those presents.

One year she decided that she would get them something which would make them think of others. She arrived with three envelopes. They thanked her and opened them – to find a leaflet from Oxfam saying they had been bought a goat. Stunned is the only word I can use for the look on their faces. 'What on earth are we going to do with a goat, and where are we going to keep it?' was the question they all asked. 'No, no you don't understand,' she replied, "these goats are for villagers in third-world countries, so they can build up a herd, and get milk and meat from them. You have so much – it's time you realised that there are people in the world who have nothing.'

I know they were aware of poverty in the world – they had certainly seen it on the television and talked about it at school – so it seemed such an odd present to give them. Later, after she had gone home, we all laughed about it, but they never forgot the Christmas when their grandmother gave them a goat each. One of the many conversations we had about it was that, surely a goat eats everything, so is it really a good idea to introduce one to a village already ravaged by drought and famine?

We did stockings for the boys and each other right up to the last Christmas we all spent together in 2008. They were a huge part of our day, and I will remember those happy children, eyes full of delight and wonder, with peals of laughter ringing around the house. Christmas will never have the same meaning for me. I don't know about this year. I think I might like to go away but Steely is adamant that we stay here. I'm not sure where I would go as the pain comes along wherever, so I guess here or away will be the same.

No stockings this year though. No more – not until we have grandchildren. If we have grandchildren. I hope we do, as it will prove that life goes on regardless. But will they too, remind us of what we cannot have, the grandchildren we will never see? I hope that when that time eventually arrives, things will not be so raw. Right now it is too painful to think of what can never be. I wonder if we will ever be able to do anything new without it equating back to three children, one lost and the 'what ifs?' and 'if onlys'. I think I'll plug myself into a bottle and hope I don't get the headache that goes with being blind drunk.

Christmas Day arrived and Rob and I woke early (we are always awake early now – sleeping is a luxury we don't have any more; a guilty pleasure if we manage a whole hour without waking in a cold sweat). We went to the cemetery and cried and wondered for the thousandth time what the hell we were doing staring at a grave that held such a precious person, far too early. There is no comfort in being there, but it's something we have to do – the only thing we can do for him now. We just go there and think and cry. Pain seeps up from the ground and engulfs us.

So many people had been and left him bits and pieces – some reindeer, some silver stars, wreaths, cards, messages of all kinds. I hate what my life has become – a series of tears, tissues and fake smiles and panic attacks that leave me feeling crap and useless, unable to function properly for days.

By the time we'd got home, both the boys were up and ready to have breakfast and presents. It was so nice that they both wanted to be here and have as normal a Christmas as possible. We ate in the late afternoon and drank a toast to Cyrus. I guess I pretended to myself that he was still in Ireland and couldn't make it back this year. Stupid, but it helped me cope with the day.

After the meal Zac, Rob and I went back up to graveside and had a drink with Cyrus – Sambuca of course. Steely had been up the day before as he didn't want going up there to become a tearful 'family' thing that we all hate – because it's just such a shit place to be. He's absolutely right and it is a place that we all hate going to, but it's also a place where Rob and I feel there is a connection – the final resting place of our son. Not a place to go every day – not for me anyway – it is too sad to do that and I don't think it actually helps or does me any good. I go when the time is right and I feel I can – and admittedly that's not necessarily every week, but then I don't think there are any rules, are there?

There are degrees of awfulness. In mathematics there is an acute angle – is that the sharpest, the most critical? I was never any good at maths but 'acute' is the awfulness I feel when at his graveside – that penetrating agony every time I see his name engraved in stone. My soul is not strong enough for that piercing on a regular basis.

New Year's Eve already; the days seem to go by and I don't really notice that one has finished and the next begun. Steely had a gig and about two hundred of the boys' friends came to watch. So many of their friends were mutual; I guess because they were all so close in age, went to the same schools and had similar tastes in people. It was a nice evening, and to be honest I'd rather have spent it with the young than on our own at home feeling old and sad. The young have it all in front of them and it's good to be able to share their hopes and watch them grow. They have been fantastic to us – and for us. I know that it has been hard for them too to have lost a friend and to watch us crumble. We try very hard to wear our smiley faces, but those who know us well understand that it's only make-up.

Elliott phoned and said that several of the squaddies wanted to come and see us on 5th January – Elliott, Moni, Willo, Reedy, Fun Time, Tommo and Marsh. We were all anxious about how would they be – how would we be, and what we would we talk about? Would it be too awful? They came from all over on the day that the country ground to a halt because of the snow. It was lovely of them to come, and they had lunch with us. The snow came down and we sat and talked, then eventually they decided it was time to go up to the cemetery. Rob gave them a bottle of champagne to take with them.

We took a back seat and didn't go, as Elliott and Marsh had been the only ones to visit his grave. For the rest of them it was the first time and we thought it right that they have this time on their own to be themselves and do what squaddies do when paying their last respects to a fallen comrade.

I wasn't sure if they would come back afterwards, but they did, having been into town and booked themselves into a hotel. It was really snowing quite hard by this time, and I was a bit worried about how on earth they were going to get back home in the morning.

At one point there was too much silence – too much not being said, and too many memories, so Rob got the air rifle out and eyes lit up – I guess soldiers will always be soldiers. The game was to shoot out the flame on a candle balanced in the rockery above the pond. They were so competitive. Gradually the target was moved further away and the hoots of laughter rang out. It was lovely, and I so wished he could have been there to see them all. I wish he wasn't just a memory.

They took Zac and Steely out in the evening, and my boys showed them the town – at least such parts of it were not closed due to snow. They managed to get kicked out of most of the pubs and have snowball fights with nearly everyone they met. They know how to play hard – they have to because they live hard. I can only imagine the things they have seen and the things that wake them up at night. You can see dark clouds in their eyes. What the hell *have* they seen? I hope they will make it through and use it to make them stronger. They all miss him. So do I. They all have stories, happy and sad; they all have memories of that dreadful day and others that followed. So do I, but mine are remote, while they were there. I hope they will be ok. And I hope they will stay in touch. I know that I need it, and I wonder if they might do too.

There is something about boys who join up. They're all slightly on the edge, which I suppose is what makes them soldiers. I can see why Cyrus was right at home with them. They are so like him in so many ways – loud, fun, fearless, fragile, loving, comradery, generous, men. I love them all for loving Cyrus the way they did. We lost a son and brother, but so did they. Some will stay within the fold of the Army, some will go. Some will go because of their injuries. I hope they all live full lives, whatever paths they take in the future.

January 13th would have been Cyrus's 20th birthday – and that was hard. He should have been here to celebrate. Why my baby; why anybody's? I know that it was what he chose to do, but I didn't choose to lose a son; I didn't choose to spend the rest of my life feeling like this. It gets harder every day, not easier. They say time heals; well it's going to take until the end of my time before I heal. I shall go with open arms when my time is up – anything to get away from this pain.

My mind is on fire and everything burns all the time – that searing pain, ripping at my flesh and making everything feel off-centre and raw. It's like having a migraine in your heart; numbing pain, blinding, crushing agony. Every second, every minute, every hour, every day is spent in physical pain.

I had thought that 2010 would bring a sense of peace, but it has just come with a slap and I feel worse. I feel sadder – if that's possible. Perhaps the initial adrenaline that keeps you going in the beginning has worn off; perhaps because the numbness has now moved and just left the festering wound of loss.

How am I supposed to go on feeling like this? I know it will be like this for the rest of my life... will I make it? It's like a cancer – the incurable kind that rots your body from the inside, making bigger and bigger holes, weaving it's malice into my very soul. Nothing anyone says will make it better. How can it? My life as I knew it is over and I really don't want this new one.

I'm so tired all the time. Every step is lead-lined. Nothing makes sense and I don't want to do anything. Even breathing is an effort. If it didn't come naturally, I don't think I'd bother to do it anymore. It's not as though I want to die, because I don't – I just don't want to feel like this any more. Where is my normal life? How can I feel so sad, every single day, and not go mad? I want to pull the duvet over my head and never come out again – eternal sleep to join you, my darling, that is what will ease this pain.

Counselling? No thank you. No-one can give me the one thing I want, so there's no point in talking to someone who didn't know him, and doesn't know me – someone who has read lots of books and might have lost an aunt to cancer. This is unfair as I know there are many counsellors and groups whose work is good and who do help a lot of people. I have been to see our doctor –though not intentionally for counselling, but only because I have an ingrowing toenail and I didn't need the added pain of this small but disabling thing. In fact he was a great help, just by being there and handing me tissue after tissue. He never offered a point of view or told me that it is all normal, this feeling of complete panic all the time.

I asked him how much the human body can cope with and he just listened to my sobs and assured me that, in fact, the human body can deal with massive trauma and is extremely resilient and mine would help to carry me through. It was all I needed to hear, at the end of the day. This is normal, my new normal. I will survive this ordeal.

The charity SSAFA (Soldiers, Sailors, Airmen and Families Association) is a group we have become a part of, although it has taken over a year for us to feel able to face families in a similar situation. Their Bereaved Family Support Group organises weekends where we, as the bereaved, can get away and feel the pressure of pretence slip away for a few hours. It is a relief to be able to relax, knowing that no-one is questioning the way you feel, whether you laugh or cry; we all have the same pain, and we all understand the agony of loss.

Rob and I attended our first SSAFA weekend in December, when we were invited to London to attend Evensong at Westminster Abbey. We travelled up by train and, after meeting with some of the other families, we walked from the hotel to the Abbey through the snow.

Rob and I were shown to our seats, which were in the pews with the choir. When they started to sing I was covered in goosebumps with the sheer power and beauty of their voices. It was an amazing experience.

After the Evensong finished, the Abbey was closed to the public and we were split into small groups and given a private tour, followed by a short ceremony and prayers around the Tomb of the Unknown Soldier. It was both incredibly moving and desperately sad.

Back at the hotel we met for dinner and spent the evening swapping stories of our soldier-sons and how we were just managing to get through each day.

There are no tools that I can use to help – no tools can bring him or my old life back, or make me feel able to be a normal person again. Coping tools can't undo what has been done. I know that they help a lot of people – brothers and sisters who will go on to have lives of their own – but mothers and fathers are broken for ever, as their future is now not what it should have been. Our futures were mapped out, but now a piece is missing and you can't read the map any more. My future was my children – it still is, but one has gone so it's not the same future.

I want Zac and Steely to go on and have their own families, and I want to be part of them but it still doesn't alter the fact that there is one missing. I don't want them to think that I don't care about them – how they feel, who they are, who they want to be. I just wish I could wave a magic wand and we could all go back to before this happened – that it had never happened.

The stinging starts at the back of my eyes. My throat goes dry and swallowing becomes difficult. Suddenly I can't breathe properly and my sight is blurred by tears. That's what happens every day. Sometimes I have to go into the downstairs loo or take the dog into the garden just so that no-one can see me cry. I'm not ashamed of crying, but sometimes the time is not right. I paint my face on every morning, and sometimes I use a little help from my make-up bag, but most of the time I just put on my imaginary 'happy' face and try and make it through the next twenty-four hours.

Rob was fifty on 5th February. What a hard day that was, watching him struggle with the whole concept of having a birthday when Cyrus is dead. It was almost suffocating – just another very sad day to add to our list of very sad days. Where do I keep all this sadness? What am I supposed to do with it? I can't seem to make it turn into anything positive – no helping myself or anyone else.

I'm not sure if I get pissed off with other people being tearful or if I just don't know how to deal with it any more. Should I be selfish and say, 'Well actually, I do mind you crying because I'm not sure who you are crying for. Is it Rob, Zac, Steely and me – or is it for yourself?' I know how much I miss him, but I'm not sure why others should say they feel the same or know how we feel. I think I'm just mixed up and not sure which way is up any more.

Work is coming to an end, and to be honest I need it to stop now. I can't take the stress of trying to deal with other's problems and having to be smiley and nice all the time. It is just such hard work and I know that sometimes my painted face cracks. People with brain injuries don't need external worries, so I'm no good for them any more. I'll miss them, but I need to go.

The other Saturday I decided to brave the journey to Cambridge. My sister had moved into a new house and had invited Mum and me for lunch. It was nice to see her new house, but to get to there I had to pass signs for Bassingbourn Barracks, where Cyrus had lived and trained for twenty weeks. That was where Rob and I dropped him off, two and a half years ago, at the start of his new life. I hadn't been in the right frame of mind before I'd left home, and once I'd arrived, having spent two hours in the car on my own and passing the barracks' signs, I felt it was maybe not such a good idea. I felt even worse and I wanted to turn around and go home – but I was there, so I couldn't.

I asked Mum if there was a route I could take to go home that would not go past Bassingbourn, because I found it so upsetting. To my dismay, she expressed surprise that I found it upsetting to drive past the barracks. I suppose Bassingbourn would have no meaning to her; although only fifteen miles from Cambridge, she never acknowledged his being there. It was becoming clear that she would never understand how I feel or be able to offer any support. That hurt, because I then understood that she is unable to be there for me as a mother figure, so I will either have to accept this or walk away. I'm doing my best to accept it, as she has been a part of my life for nearly fifty years. Perhaps it's just old age and living on your own for too long. I hope I never get like that. I would like to think that my children have always known that they and Rob are the most important things in my life, and that I would do anything to protect and support them – even though I know I'm not the same mother or partner that I was before all this happened. I can't ever go back to that person. She is lost forever.

When you touch the antennae of a snail it folds and disappears into itself. That's how I feel some days. I just want to retreat into the womb and make the world go away. That butterfly feeling in my stomach returns, making me feel sick and fragile all the time. My mother should be my 'womb' but that is just a wish; like wishing for things to be different. So, just another wish unfulfilled.

CHAPTER 13

CORPORAL RICHARD GREEN

Another Rifleman from Reading was killed last week in Afghanistan.

How small this world truly is! We had seen him standing outside the church on the day of Cyrus's funeral, and I knew he was a soldier, even though he wasn't in uniform. Standing so tall and proud – they have an air about them. How terrible that he should be killed, exactly nine months after Cyrus.

Nine; now that's a hard number. Nine months I carried him, nineteen years I loved him, nurturing him, watching him grow. Nine months since I lost him. Nearly a year since I last saw his eyes open. Where has that time gone? What do I do when I get to that anniversary? I'll never get to hold him, touch him, talk to him, laugh with him, cry with him. I truly believe that no-one should ever have to feel this pain.

We're going to Richard Green's funeral on Tuesday. I'm not sure if the boys will come, as I know they need to sort things out at their own pace and another funeral in the same church might not be the way to do it. I know that they want to show their respect for Richard – but at what price to themselves?

I feel sick already, and I've not even decided what to wear. Can I wear the same outfit? Will it scald like it did the first time I wore it? How do I go and sit through their pain and not be completely immersed in my own? Am I selfish or is it the natural way of things?

I didn't cry in the church when Cyrus's coffin was there. I only cried when they lowered him into the ground. We'll not go to the cemetery this time. I can't look at that open wound in the ground – not again, not even for someone else's coffin. Too much pain and anguish goes with that. I know I'll cry when I see Richard's coffin in the church, but I'm completely aware that my tears will be for Cyrus and the loss we suffer. I also know that wrapped up with those tears will be the pain that I feel for Richard's friends and family. That ache that never goes, that pain behind eyes I don't know, those muffled sobs that I heard last June, the agony of losing someone you love and the inability to comprehend what has happened.

All these feelings and more – I've been practising them all weekend; the catch in the throat, the sting in the eye, the nauseating headache that I've not managed to shake for over nine months. So close to home and yet…

They didn't know each other but their lives were intertwined and now they'll rest together, with those other young men and women who had a vision and followed it. It's those of us left behind who have to try to understand that vision and how it all fits together. I don't think for one moment that they believed they would leave us so soon, or that they had any idea of the broken people they would leave behind.

I feel like a smashed plate, splintered in a thousand pieces. I wish, like the chemical element mercury, it were possible to pull myself back together – but I suppose that even if I did, there would still be missing pieces making me a shadow of my former self.

I hate having to pretend. It's sometimes like a game. I pretend I'm fine and getting on with things, when in reality I'm not. I feel so much worse – that river pulls me down, through darker and darker passages. It's always so cold. I'm always so cold. I feel as though I've lost the ability to feel normal things any more. I laugh, but it's not me. I talk, but it's not me. Who is this person sitting at this blank page, putting down words that are confused and hurtful? Who have I become?

I drink to numb the pain, but it just makes me feel worse. I don't sleep without dreaming or tossing and turning, trying to get my new skin to fit and feel comfortable. Those sores open up and ooze at night. Evil creeps in and sits in my head. The evil of a life altered, the evil of a family thrust into a world they have no wish to be a part of – the evil of broken everything.

The other day I read the poems of a self-harmer. How cruel we are to one another. Why, when such dreadful things happen anyway, would we deliberately want to hurt someone we know? Her words rang so true, even though she was writing about something completely different. Her pain at the unjustness of life and others struck a chord. Pain and suffering is shared by so many, and yet we don't see it – or if we do, we chose to ignore it. Does it make those not in pain feel power? Is the pushing down of others the thing that elevates? Does that elevation make them feel good about themselves? I can't bear all this pain and yet I can understand the need to inflict it upon oneself, just to release the pressure. The feeling I have of being trapped in a life I can't move on from is so frightening that I feel that the letting of my blood might possibly ease that feeling of needing to explode.

We move through this life so selfishly. Children are selfish, old people are selfish –and all those ages in between are too. I want; stamp, stamp. I need; scream, scream. We are so wrapped up in our own selfishness that we don't see the needs of others. I see and yet I can't help. Is this because the most dreadful thing has happened – or do I just think I have the power to see because of it? Selfish? I guess I am.

Richard's father spoke at the funeral of being an ordinary family that extraordinary things just didn't happen to. Well, some of us are lucky enough to have extraordinary children (not just those who join the forces) but children who touch people's lives and make them better people. I have one of those families, and perhaps Richard came from one too.

They are together now, side by side, soldier-like in the small military plot at the cemetery. It is strange seeing other people's flowers and words. People we don't know – but whom I suppose over the coming months we might get to know. I don't often go up there and meet people but the other day Rob and I went to see Cyrus and Richard too, and there were four of Cyrus's friends there. Odd – no not odd, just unusual to be there at the same time. The last time I saw anyone since was on Remembrance Sunday I think – but I'm not sure no day has a beginning or an end any more.

I'm not sure how I feel about it all. We have spent nine months going to visit Cyrus's grave and it being in the middle on its own. Now Richard is buried no more than two feet from him and even though I know it is right and proper and I have no doubt in my mind that it is exactly where he should be, it seems strange. Two lots of flowers now, two lots of people mourning the death of a loved one. Both Riflemen, both young, both having chosen their paths knowing the risks and still prepared to take them.

Do I feel slightly resentful? That's an awful thought, because deep down of course I don't. I guess I'd just got used to having the place to ourselves. Selfish. How selfish! I didn't want to have to share this space – but then again, I didn't want any other family to have to wade through this glue. Now the space is less, there are more flowers again, tributes to a hero, last messages to a loved one. Oh God, this shouldn't be happening. It opens up those old wounds that had never really healed, but only been covered by others fighting for space in a heart that seems unable to refuse entry.

I suppose we had got to a point where we reached 'phase two'. The headstone had gone up and we were just waiting for the turf to go down. Now we have to watch Richard's flowers fade and someone else will have to make the painful decision of when to throw them away. We will have to watch as the ground sinks. That in itself is an agony, even though you know in your head the coffin is still intact your heart tells you it's collapsing (which of course it isn't). Then their phase two will come with the erection of his headstone. I wonder what words they will have inscribed on it. The Rifles emblem will be the same. The K I A (killed in action) is the same – just the date, name, age, rank and personal message will be different. We tried to keep it simple and relevant to anyone civilian or military that wanted to visit and feel that the message was personal to them, I hope it works:

30011938 Rifleman
Cyrus Thatcher
2nd Battalion The Rifles
2nd June 2009 Aged 19
K I A in Afghanistan
Forever in our hearts

Same glue, same darkness, different family. Sad days to add to the collection I already have. It's not the sort of treasured collection you pass down to the next generation.

Another brave young man, who loved his job and was so obviously good at it – he must have been to be only twenty-three, and already a corporal.

So many things make me cry. The blush of spring flowers in the garden, a song or the tone of a voice on the radio, stroking a dog that I know Cyrus would have loved. Some days all these things just seem to make the pain stronger. I wish I knew how to control it, then I could eke it out in small doses so that I didn't feel as though I was going to choke on it all the time.

It sneaks up and hits me from behind; just when I think I've had a couple of days without it and that perhaps I'll make it through a whole week, it bites me, leaving gouges that feel like they're lined with acid.

Come and gone the anniversary of the last time I saw him. That was the day of Richard's funeral. How can a year have gone so fast when so much of it has been filled with the agony of loss? Some days I feel as though I've always lived this life of tears and pain. How to explain that to people – and do they really need to know? No, I don't think so – no-one really wants to know. I guess another metaphor is that my grief is like a spring shower; sudden and heavy but then gone and blue sky all in the space of five minutes. Odd.

CHAPTER 14

HOLLOW
LAUGHTER

Some people manage to channel their grief into the energy to do something positive. I don't have that energy. I sometimes wish I could immerse myself in helping others who have suffered loss, or experienced the things that soldiers do, but at the moment I can't. Selfishness raises its ugly head again – selfish but not uncaring. I care deeply about the lot of others, but I'm unable to drag myself out of my own self-pity to help them yet. Who knows, I may never be able to do it. There seems so little energy these days – lack of motivation, lack of passion, lack of everything.

I fear my inability to let go of Zac and Steely. Zac worries about leaving us, and I worry about him worrying. Steely wants to escape, but I need him to need me – all of it destructive perhaps, or natural. I don't know any more, I'm not in control. How do I let my children move on without making them too scared to do it? What tools do I give them, when I can't use any of the ones I've got? I know the natural course life should take, but our lives have been shunted into another one and I don't know the way.

I feel like Gretel, dropping crumbs and hoping they will be there to show me the way back. I know the outcome of dropping those crumbs, but it doesn't stop me doing it anyway. So much of my life seems to be made up of metaphors, most of which I'm sure have been used before. Perhaps I've heard them somewhere, and now I need to use them myself.

I've just finished reading a book called 'Kisses on a Postcard' about evacuees during the Second World War. Whole communities were affected by loss, and I wonder if they dealt with it differently – or was it such a common occurrence to lose someone or know someone who had? They seemed to have a resilience I can't muster. Was it that their lives were so much tougher in the first place, and I've been spoilt by modern life – the 'must have' society that we seem to live in now? I wish I had some of their grit and determination. I wish I were as tough as my children seem to be.

Today the sky is the colour of Cyrus's favourite blue jumper. The spring flowers are creating a yellow blush across the country – and I don't care. Everything is wrong. How can the sky be such a reminder of what I don't have any more? Perhaps if I were blind I would feel differently. I wouldn't have to look at people's 'sad' eyes or watch them look away because they dare not look too closely.

Self-pity is not pretty, and that's what I'm wading through this morning. Sticky, clawing, invasive and murdering – that's what self-pity is today. I know I need to move on, but I can't today. Perhaps tomorrow will be different.

When I have to look at myself in the mirror, there are so few outward signs that anything is wrong. There are perhaps more lines around my eyes and slight shadowing under them. My neck has 'turkey skin' as the boys call it, and I look awful in a polo neck these days – but unless you have the ability to read people's eyes, I don't think anyone would ever guess... unless they knew. There are some days when I look worse than others. Rob too has days when his skin is greyish and he just looks exhausted, as though he's not slept for weeks. Mind you, neither of us sleeps well.

My dreams have returned – not the gory ones that made me wake in a sweat, but those that still wake me wet from tears. The feeling of doom in the middle of the night has not gone, and I suppose it will take years to go. Lying awake reliving all the awful moments – moments when we had to tell everyone; moments when we had to wait for the plane to land; moments when we had to see our child lying dead in a coffin; all those moments that, no matter how hard I try to erase them, glide through my thoughts and poison them.

The only person who understands me completely is Rob. This nightmare is ours, and together we've faced the worst – together we will survive this. We gauge each other's mood, and even if the moods are opposite, we meet in the middle, adjusting them to suit. We're in this together. There is no, 'I'm feeling worse than you,' or 'Why are you in a bad mood?' We're equally devastated. If we laugh there is no guilt in that laugh, as we both know the agony underneath it. If we cry, our sorrow is shared. I don't know if I could have come this far without him.

The photos hurt. Dusting them always makes me cry – not the ones with him in uniform so much, as he didn't wear it at home so I don't really equate him with khaki. It's the ones of Rob and the boys in Turkey at the baths, covered in mud. Holding up crabs they'd caught in rock pools on the beach in Devon. Cyrus standing on our drive in front of a blue Rolls Royce that he'd organised and paid for. The owner was someone he'd delivered morning paper to over the years, and he'd knocked on his door and asked if he could pay him to take himself and his friend Charlotte to the School Prom. He offered £50 and we always presumed this had been accepted because of his audacity – or perhaps it was that irresistible smile. It's the photos that we have scattered throughout the house – those are the ones that make me catch my breath.

Last Sunday we reached the eleven-month mark. How could eleven months go so fast? And yet it all seems like several lifetimes ago that those men walked up our drive. Most of 2009 was spent in a blur. We've been left a legacy of sadness and I don't want it. I can't share it, I can't rid myself of it, and can't help anyone else with it.

Maggie tells me that time will change how I feel, but not stop the pain – just dull it. How much time? Forever, I guess. Every day of every year until I die. I don't want that, but it's now my lot. Can I, with this weight around my heart, help others move on? I don't want them to feel the burden of my pain; I just want to help them free themselves of theirs.

I worry about Zac hiding himself away from his friends, but I know what he means when he says, 'They don't understand.' I also know that they can help him by being a distraction, even if it's only for a short while. After all, a distraction is a distraction. However hard it is for us and Zac, their lives go on and they will never know what it is like – but I also realise that they want to help. People mean well, but when you are in such a lonely place, no-one can really reach you until you push through it, take a deep breath and step forward.

I've shared thoughts with people on the radio and in the papers, but those are my public thoughts. The private ones are buried deep, and honestly people don't really want to know those.

Next week we have been invited to Prince Edward's Garden Party next at Bagshot Park with its gardens and halls – with the bereaved and seriously injured. I wonder if any of the soldiers from 10 Platoon will be there, and how their lives have been over the past eleven months. They too have secret places in their heads – too secret to share, as the average person would not be able to handle the scenes they keep there.

On Monday we planted hundreds of poppy seeds in our garden. They will always remind me of Cyrus and all those thousands of white gravestones with words of love carved into them. Crazy how a flower can make you cry. I think it's because the petals are so delicate, tissue paper thin, vulnerable like the human body and yet purposeful and beautiful. Just like the human body.

We met in a hall at Sandhurst, with all the other families – some with young children, some faces familiar some not. I wonder if it's more difficult to live with the young who don't understand, or the old. I'm not sure how I would behave if I had young children – children who didn't really know him and wouldn't share the agony of having lost him. They would grow up never really understanding the sorrow of losing something so precious.

It was not the sort of gathering where you can waltz up to someone and say, Hello, is your son dead or injured? So we stood there in limbo, listening to the murmuring of voices but not able to catch a whole sentence – not that I'd much to say to anyone anyway. The only other family I felt any kinship towards was the Mervises, and they were not there yet. I wondered if they would come.

As we were moved towards the buses that would take us to Bagshot Park, Margaret and Jonathan arrived. It was lovely to see them – I felt at ease with them. They remained my connection to all that has happened, although I couldn't really explain why.

We arrived through large gates and drove past huge rhododendron hedges – not many flowers as it had been a strange spring and most flowers seemed to have gone already. Then the house came into view. The buses parked on a large circular drive in front of a rather lovely red brick manor house – not huge, not over posh, just a nice, attractive country house and gardens. We were greeted by staff and given maps of the gardens. There were several trails through them and even though it was quite cold, we set off in little groups. We joined the Mervises for a while, and this gave Margaret and me a chance to catch up briefly.

We parted and Rob, the boys and I went up towards the Orangery which is, or could be, such a lovely old building. However, there is no money in the coffers for this costly repair and anyway, no one but Prince Edward and his family would benefit from it, so sadly it stands in disrepair. One of the garden staff asked if we've been up to the swing, so we followed a grassy path up through lovely pine trees of unfathomable age until the path opened up, and there was a lady standing beside a wooden swing. We approached, and she told us it was the Queen's grandchildren's swing. 'Could we have a go on it?' we asked. 'Only if you don't tell anyone – mind you it would be fun to say that you'd swung on the Queen's grandchildren's swing.' she replied.

Zac went first while Steely pushed, then jumped off it as it was high on its forward arc. Steely then sat on it and Zac pushed – and he too jumped off, but was not as fortunate with his landing and ended up rolling down the hill. We did laugh, which was strange as it wasn't the sort of day when you felt that you ought to be laughing. In fact, there have actually not been any days when I've felt it right to laugh since Cyrus was killed. The only funny part was that we were all dressed up in our 'Sunday best' and Steely had got grass stains on his knees and elbows.

A buffet was served in the house, during which we were to meet Prince Edward. Two dogs were roaming around and they acted as a distraction – everything was very odd. We were to meet Prince Edward, the Royal attached to 2 Rifles who has an awful lot to do with them regarding the injured, I believe. I was not sure what to expect – should we stand and bow?

He then appeared from a doorway slightly to our right and spent a few minutes at each of the tables (there were some hundred and fifty people attending). He was dressed in corduroys and a tweed jacket and was actually much slighter than I'd imagined. Then he approached our table and shook our hands – he was quite humble and quietly spoken. He said he was so very sorry – but what could we say in reply – 'Thank you'? I've never been quite sure what sort of thing I'm supposed to say to that. We moved on to neutral territory to save embarrassment, and we asked about the dogs. It was weird, but I'd no idea what to say to him and he really was at a loss as to what to say to us because, in the face of it, nothing is really quite right.

He moved to the next table and we continued with our sandwiches and cakes. Before we left there was time to go around the gardens again. We walked around the house, which was just as beautiful from the front or back, whichever way you look at it. It was a lovely, understated house that you could feel really was a home – but I just didn't want to be there for the reason we were – but then without that reason I'd not be there anyway.

As we stood on a slight hill overlooking a large ornamental pond, Captain Andy Pemberton and the new colonel (who has taken over from Colonel Rob Thomson), whose name I've forgotten but who seemed very nice and surprisingly young looking, came up towards us, with what looked like a large photo under him arm. It was a framed certificate and medal that he presented to us on behalf of ISAF (International Security Assistance Force), for the time that Cyrus served in Kosovo.

Another medal – another reminder that he wasn't there to receive it himself. He would have so loved these medals. How do you react when you're supposed to be so proud – but all it does is twist the knife in a little further? It is an honour I know, but it should be his not ours – not one more thing to add to the little corner in the sitting room above his wooden chest. It just hurts.

We were loaded on to the buses again and headed back to Sandhurst to pick up the car. Matt Wilson (Willo) sat beside us to the right and Paul Jacobs (who had been blinded by a blast, been awarded the George Medal for bravery, and who had asked Margaret Mervis to be his advocate) sat in front, while Zac and Steely sat behind us. There was some banter on the way and laughter from both Matt and Paul, but what struck me most was the hollowness of that laughter. It was a show – not deliberate, but a show to the world that all was well, even though one was blind and one had only one leg. The laughter was so chilling that it has remained with me. One more sign of how this has affected these boys; one more thing they have to learn to do. I paint on my smile; they perfect their hollow laughs. Perhaps if you'd not known their circumstances it would have seemed like a good-natured ride on a bus, but to me it was frightening to listen to. Had he lived, would Cyrus have perfected this laugh and learnt to apply his make-up?

Later that evening, as Rob and I talked about the day, the conversation turned to Paul Jacobs, both of us realising we'd seen him in one of the photos Cyrus had taken in Afghanistan while in FOB Gibraltar, Helmand Province. He was sitting on the dusty ground, knees bent up, holding a small brown and white puppy that must have barely been ten weeks old.

Forward Operating Base Gibraltar was the name given to the secured military base they used to support tactical operations and Cyrus had taken many photos. Together with his letters, they gave us an insight into their lives in the FOB – their cramped sleeping quarters, operation and communication rooms, the pipes dug into the ground used as urinals.

> *Afghanistan – 1st May 2009*
> *If you saw what and where I've been sleeping you would be shocked!! So pictures will back me up! Unfortunately 3 blokes died 2 days ago in an IED explosion in one of the FOBs 'bout 2 kilometers away – we visited that FOB 2 days before the attack – fucking mental – quite scary actually!*

Images of the sand-bagged walls they rested against, smoking, preparing before they went out on patrol. The same walls whose shadows they sat in to keep cool while they cleaned their weapons. Meals of goat that the Afghan Army had slaughtered and shared with those hungry enough to try it. Quad bikes and equipment, and dust blown up by the Chinooks bringing supplies, welfare parcels and letters from home.

> *Afghanistan – 12th May 2009*
> *Hello Mother,*
> *Yesterday was a massive day for morale, an American chopper came in. URGE people to send photos – they keep morale SKY HIGH. I thought Steely and Zac's (poses) in the garden were quality. I can only prove how much a letter or*

> *small parcel means by finding the time to write back – that's probley the most precious thing I have and I'd trade hours for a letter.*
>
> *I can't explain how good it is to get pictures and stuff. You get grown men close to tears at the sight of their kid or a good night out – it's really strange how this place fucks with your head and emotions.*

During one of the rare occasions he was able to phone, he commented on how close they were to the Taliban – he estimated 600 metres away while in the FOB, and that there had been times on patrol that they could hear bullets cutting through the air just centimetres above their heads. He was amazed that no-one from 10 Platoon had been killed.

Only two weeks now until the anniversary of that awful day. Two weeks – and it's the same feeling of dread that I had before Christmas. How would the day pan out? What do we do? Will I feel it's just another normal day in my now abnormal life? How do others cope? How would I ask? Who would I ask? I know that we are not alone in this, but it seems it. That twist of fate that has led us to this awful day. One step in another direction and we'd not be here. One step, oh Cyrus. Step by dreadful step, we move through this newly created life. It might be a year, but it is still new, fresh, daunting – agonisingly difficult. I stumble through it now. Stumbling steps.

They came knocking at our door again, those soldiers, this time to mark the anniversary – a year to the day they last saw him alive. Those young men whose lives have also been turned upside down by all of this. It is always with slight apprehension that I greet them at the door. How are they? How are they coping? Will we be able to talk normally and have a conversation that isn't studded with long pauses and ghosts?

We had lunch and it was hot, so we sat in the garden. Last time they were here it was snowing, just to prove, I guess, that life goes on like the seasons. At one point Rob was in the kitchen on his own and Elliott joined them. They talked for ages, and I think it was what Elliott needed to do. I hope it helped him a little. I knew it wasn't for me to join in – my presence would have stopped the conversation cold, and I didn't want that to happen. He is so sad, that boy. He misses him so much. We all do, but they had a friendship that only comes along once or twice in a lifetime. I so wish they had had more time together. Cyrus's life was too short for so many people and for so many reasons.

By mid-afternoon they needed to get going. They'd been given an extra day's leave to come to see us and they needed to get back to Ireland, so they went up to the grave and then made their way back to airports and train stations. In the end they were a distraction – they made the day go faster and they helped us, and I hope it helped them a little too. It is so sad though – they miss him so much. When they tell stories, their eyes light up, but then the reality hits again and they mist over and go back to those blank exhausted eyes we saw in November.

Elliott is in a place I can't reach. How do you cope at that age when those who surround you are unable to help with the nightmares, loneliness, anger, guilt, sorrow and pain? I know it is how Zac and Steely feel too.

These lads, like Zac and Steely, are boys still, dressed in men's clothing – but still boys at heart. They need to be held and told that it will be ok. I'll always love them all for being such friends to Cyrus and for wanting desperately to help us in some way. They will all always have a place in my heart, and I hope their ghosts fade, leaving them able to move forward – not to forget, but move towards a future.

Rob and I went up to the cemetery at 6.30 to meet friends. On the way we saw groups of Cyrus's friends whom we'd just missed at the cemetery. They waved and made their way down to the pub on the corner. I knew we were welcome to join them, but it somehow doesn't seem right to be in a pub drinking, talking and laughing – not yet we're not ready. We may never be ready. There were many others at graveside, and judging by the amount of flowers, cards, bottles of drink and cigarettes left for him, it was apparent there had been a constant stream of people throughout the day. I was very touched. I have this irrational fear he will be forgotten by those friends left behind. I know this isn't true, but in my darkest hours, doubt rears its ugly head, bringing me to my knees, time and again. We all hugged, kissed, cried and thanked them for being there, knowing there was no need for thanks – but we said it anyway. It was the same with any greeting; people falling into the ritual of politeness: 'Hello, how are you?' or 'All right, mate?' We were all guilty of it – it was such a ridiculous thing to ask under the circumstances.

Looking back, the day went in a blur. Like so many days this past year, it merged into another one, and pushed us towards the next. I can't believe we've gone through all the seasons and have come back to the start again. It's frightening how times goes by and you don't realise.

More nightmares last night. It seems such a long time since I dreamt of Cyrus. This was a dark, damp, cold dream where everyone was going to die or had died but they kept on marching past. Grey men, grey uniforms, no hope. I woke several times in a cold sweat and in tears, only to fall asleep again and continue the dream. I felt like shit this morning. All I wanted to do was crawl into a space where the nightmares couldn't find me and sleep for a hundred years. Why is the brain so cruel? Why now, after weeks, do I have to have these visions and feel the touch of his soft face, knowing that it's not real and that I have to wake and face the reality of a life without one of my children? Where are those cool hands that caressed and soothed the pain away? As a mother I used to do that – but not any more. My hands are hot and scratchy, and they leave deep grooves of pain and sorrow. They're not able to heal any more.

I put dark red lipstick on this morning. I don't know why, but it felt right. A gash of red on my face somehow seemed appropriate today. It was going to be a bad day, today. I could already feel it, working its way through my brain and I couldn't stop it – it has a mind of its own.

I feel like the Joker – all white paint and an angry gash of red; that Heath Ledger madness with crazed eyes and affected brain. He was brilliant in that film, and he too never made it to old age.

I've never been to an Arboretum – didn't even known what one was – but there we were being driven up the motorway towards Staffordshire. Debbie, my school friend and her husband Dave came with us, steering us in the direction of yet another stifling day of grief.

We had been invited to go to a ceremony with all those families who had lost someone in Afghanistan in 2009. Each year the names of all those who have fallen the previous year are carved into the massive curved stone walls of the memorial and Cyrus's name was added along with the other one hundred and eight who were killed in 2009.

I saw that haunted look again that day. Not in my own eyes (I've got used to that now), but in the eyes of other families who don't understand what is happening and what has happened. So many names, so many broken families and so much sorrow and pain. Today we are among the five hundred privately invited mourners. Five hundred, lost and confused, left to wonder what it was all supposed to be about – this agony that we share. So many people sobbed when they heard a name they recognised being called out – a roll call of the dead. Names added to the sixteen thousand who have died since World War II. I don't think very many people actually realised how many have gone since then; to the general public they have gone unnoticed – just a headline one day and fish-and-chip paper the next. Cruel, but true. But then life is cruel.

After the ceremony we sat, Rob, Dave, Debbie and I, at a table with another set of parents. Their son had been killed by a blast on New Year's Eve – but no day is a good day to lose a child. The father asked Rob if it got any easier with time. What could he say? The truth is no – in fact it gets harder. Should you say this, or do you let them find out for themselves? Rob just told him the truth; that he found every day hard, no day easier or harder than another – all hard and uncompromising. Not what they really wanted to hear; but I suspected that they already knew this. I'd already been told by Maggie months ago that the pain never lessens – you just get used to it – so I suppose I'd been prepared in a sense. Don't expect this to go away, it will just change. No amount of time will heal; time just allows you to get used to a new constant.

On Saturday it will be a year since Paul Mervis was killed. What can I say to Margaret? There is nothing. I will send her an e-mail letting her know that we are thinking of them – not that I don't think of them every day. Cyrus's and Paul's deaths seem to have gone hand in hand, and we share this common hole in our hearts. It's one we share with so many others, but for some reason I feel closer to Margaret than others. So strange to end up having a fondness for and becoming friends with someone whom I would probably have never met if our sons hadn't been killed. Such nice people – such a dreadful outcome.

I sometimes wonder if there is an afterlife. It would be so nice to see them all again – hold them, stroke their hair, hear their voices, see their smiles. It would be lovely, but I just don't know. I see images of earth from outer space, so where is the heaven? Does it hide behind some solar system, way out there in the black? I can't picture what it would be like. Perhaps if I believed it would be different – of course it would... I'd believe. No, for me there is no heaven, a place where things are so much better than here and now. Why would we need to be here at all if the outcome was heaven? What would be the point of any of this? Are we all to spend eternity in white, looking peaceful and smiley? I just can't seem to get a grip of that image. I know some do, and that's good – but not for me I'm afraid.

Surely one day I'll run out of tears. I can understand how time might heal if you lose a partner. You can, if you're lucky, fall in love again. We can never have another Cyrus. So time healing is a myth made up by those who have never lost a child. A white lie told to help you move on. We can't move on – we just move along, and there is a huge difference. I hope next year we will be able to say we have moved on a little... who knows?

I wish I could put my finger on what it is that makes some days worse than others. I do have better days, but I also know that these days are, at present, few and far between. I also know on a bad day that it will change again, and become not such a bad day. Perhaps this is how those who are bi-polar feel; never quite able to relax because you know it can change as quickly as a thought flicking across your mind.

Black holes are all consuming, I've been told. Perhaps grief is a black hole. Cold, vast, uncompromising, and empty without end. I would love to be able to go back to having the life I had with no black holes – just hope and joy. The hope and joy of the young, not the worry that our young now have, wondering if we, as parents, will cope with life if they move on to have lives of their own. I don't want them to feel that pressure, the pressure of responsibility. It is not theirs to have yet – they need their own children for that. There are still so many things I wish for.

Should I care that they are thinking of pulling the troops out of Sangin? It won't make any difference to our life. I suppose that it might stop others having to go through this, but for me personally it makes no difference. Soldiers go where they are told to – where they are needed – and if the need moves, so do they. It's all political jiggery-pokery – vote-conscious men trying to win hearts and minds. I don't want to be involved in the political side of grief. I have enough trouble dealing with my day-to-day ability to cope, let alone worry about where our troops are now.

There are five stages of grief, or so I'm told. Only five? Surely not. Surely every second of every day is a stage. It's not a red-lipstick-day today – more like a sloppy, slovenly day when my hair is unwashed and my socks don't match. Those are my stages of grief. Everyday things, such as not being bothered to cook because everything tastes like sawdust – so what's the point? The dog has chewed another stick into a thousand pieces so I'll need to get the Hoover out again. Those are my stages of grief – things that happen without being noticed – subtle changes in mood, facial expression, tissues used and stuffed into pockets.

It's not easy to go through and, I guess, not easy to witness. I went to Cambridge on Monday to have a belated birthday lunch for my sister Mione, at Mum's house. Mione has in fact, been one of our only relatives constant in her approach to this whole awful business.

I understand why I feel animosity towards certain friends and my mother. It is because they have what I don't, and I know now I have anger, and the need to direct it at someone or something. I realise now that it has been my mother who has taken the brunt of this, but I mustn't compare myself as a mother to how she is as a mother. There is no comparison. There is no blame to be had, either. I know that neither she nor anyone could have changed this situation and I must not confuse my feelings of hurt in the past with the pain I feel now. I get a sharp pain across my shoulders, and I want to erect a wall around myself, when I think about having to face them, have a normal conversation, pretend that I'm doing well... getting on and feeling better.

It's rather like sitting behind a bullet-proof screen. I can have a conversation through it, but their breath doesn't reach my nostrils, and if they put their hands up towards me there is no feeling of touch there any more, just the space in between our flesh. Nothing, an empty space where there used to be kinship and trust.

Is my change in attitude obvious? Do I send out visible signals? I don't think so, as I have a feeling they are unaware of how I feel. I have learnt to put on my make-up well. If I told them the truth it would hurt, and I don't want to do that. I just feel completely remote. I have to pretend that I'm interested in what they are doing and how they are feeling, and I feel guilty at that – and yet I'm unable to stop it. They too have felt the pain of Cyrus's death; perhaps that is what makes me feel like this. It is my pain, not to be shared – but that of course, is completely untrue and even writing it makes me blush. But sometimes that's what I want to scream at them. They have no right to look sad or think they understand how I feel – how we feel.

Is it a photograph that triggers a memory, or a memory that makes you search out that photograph?

All the photos are of a smiling boy who looked as if he didn't have a care in the world. Those lovely smiling eyes... I miss them so much. It's like being slammed into a wall, sudden, painful, hard, and cold – all those things and so much more. Words are so inadequate.

It is human nature to want to retreat and lick our wounds. How many sores can I heal with the patient lick of a raspy tongue? Can a lick fix the very fibre of our souls – and would we want it fixed? If it's fixed, is it forgotten? I don't want to forget – I just don't want to be here in the first place. This place of darkness, moss-covered walls that seep sorrow and anguish. Looking up, there is no speck of light – no warmth or comfort. I'm just left alone in the dark.

I wonder if this is how my friend Jane felt when her husband had a brain haemorrhage and her world fell to pieces. Did she feel this helpless and hopeless? Was I one of the people she felt she couldn't reach any more? Had we been too close, shared too many secrets, laughed too loudly before the world as we knew it ended? Was it my punishment for daring to have a normal life that carried on when hers was so obviously ruined? Strange how we have drifted back into friendship; I don't truly believe it ever really went away, but now oddly, we share a common bond again – our changed lives. We both have changed lives we had never planned for or envisaged ourselves leading; we now have a bond too strong to break again – a bond borne of tragedy.

So many lost opportunities of death; lost child, lost grandchildren, lost laughter, lost love, the lost life of one so young and so full of promise. We are a sum total of all those who have touched our lives, even on the fringes.

I am who I am because I had a son who was Cyrus, because I have children who are Zac and Steely, because I'm in love with Rob. They are who I am, not the things I wish I had or the people I wish I'd known.

CHAPTER 15

THE INQUEST

We have some good family friends, Marcel and Sally Wagner who, together with Shiplake College, Henley-on-Thames, organise a month-long expedition to Kenya each year, for the sixth form. Included in these trips are climbing Mount Kenya, white-water rafting on the Athi and Tana rivers, safaris, camping, and trekking in the Chyulu Hills. They have also formed a special Schools Project with Kikunduku School, raising money for uniforms, books and equipment.

Marcel asked Zac if he would like to join them, knowing he would be an asset to the trip and the Schools Project would be grateful for his building skills.

Armed with an extensive equipment list, Rob and Zac spent several evenings rooting through Rob's survival kit – rucksacks, walking boots, waterproof bags and mosquito nets. There were two things Zac packed that weren't on the list; one was a hip-flask containing some Sambuca, and the other was a 2 Rifles wristband – a khaki-coloured rubber strap embossed in dark green letters is 2 RIFLES Afghanistan 09 – Swift and Bold. We, as a family, have all worn these wristbands since Cyrus first went to Afghanistan, and now none of us can take them off. Over the months we've sold many to friends and family, raising money for the 2 Rifles Benevolent Fund.

The trek up Mount Kenya takes six days and when Zac reached the summit he took out his hipflask, toasted Cyrus, then climbed to the top of a flagpole that has been put there, and slid the wrist-band over the top.

It was during this trip that he met Mark Savage, who runs the White-Water Rafting Company that, coincidently, is used by the Army for R & R after they have been on training exercises in Kenya. Whilst talking with Mark, Zac learned that 2 Rifles were due there in September. Cyrus would have loved it.

When they arrived at Kikunduku School they were greeted by hordes of dancing and singing men, women and children. Some danced with wooden guns and the women had made themselves belts out of bottle tops that jingled as they danced. Later that afternoon a Kenyan tribal banquet was laid on, and the main course was goat. How strange that while Cyrus was in Afghanistan, he too had a banquet of goat. I don't know if either of them thought about it, and I don't expect for a minute my mother meant to do it – but they did get that Christmas present she'd given them all those years ago. Your day will come too, Steely.

The next day, Zac and some of the boys from Shiplake College unpacked large amounts of wood that had been purchased with some of the money raised. They set up an assembly line building desks, and soon there was a crown of wide-eyed children. Zac has a way about him

– he is softly spoken, kind and has infinite patience when it comes to showing people how to do things. The tools used to put the desks together were a novelty to the children, so Zac explained with sounds and actions how to use a saw without bloodshed and hammer in nails without bruising any fingers. 'Smooth,' he would say, as he used the saw. 'Smooth, smooth,' repeated a whispering chorus of children. 'Flush,' when joining two pieces of wood, and again, 'Flush, flush,' they'd repeat. He came back brown and refreshed, and I'm glad he went. I hope, if the opportunity arises, he will go back to Mount Kenya and the Schools Project.

It is tragic that Cyrus can't be here to compare stories of African adventures with Zac, and be here to see Steely grow into a man, and go off to start a new life in America.

The summer is coming to a close and so too another chapter of our lives. Soon we board an aeroplane headed for Los Angeles; Steely to a new life at the Musicians Institute (MI) in Hollywood where he will be studying the drums – something he has aspired to since he first picked up a drumstick at the age of thirteen – going to America and becoming the best, surrounded by the best and competing against the best. The rest of us back at home in England head towards more uncertainty of what's to come. There is that mixture of pleasure and pain. Pleasure at the leap Steely is taking in attaining his new life, – one I hope will be filled with laughter, and all the experiences adventure can push his way – and pain at another son leaving home. I know that this is completely different, but the feeling of life changing and being unable to stop it doesn't. I do need life to change; the boys need to move onwards and upwards. They are free to fly, and we as parents are the launching pad. Their lives are just beginning – we are part of that, but in the span of a lifetime (one of great age I hope) we are such a small piece in the picture they have yet to complete.

I must try and curb the rising panic in my throat – the need to hold him and never let go, even though I know I must. The dry catch of my heart, its beat irregular, pounding out the minutes and hours until we have to say goodbye, punching at the walls of my soul and enveloping me in glue all over again at the thought of losing another son. Even the knowledge that this is different doesn't help. It's because I've seen the reality – I know what it is like to lose someone you love – which makes my love for Zac and Steely almost smothering. It is the constant fear of loss. He will leave another empty space, even though it is a positive one.

I know too that I must not crush Zac in my need to hold on to the new 'normal' that the past months have become. He too must be allowed to find his own niche, experience all life can and will throw at him. Grow, move on, have his own complete life; one that has changed but one that will, hopefully with time, be filled with joy and the smiles I know have been temporarily lost. And, I hope, will prove that there is a life out there to be had for all of us.

Los Angeles was hot and busy. Rather like living life on the M25 – constant movement, constant noise. Steely will love it, I'm sure. Now to the task at hand, to find him accommodation, meet the staff at MI, sort out his Health Insurance (thank goodness for the NHS – we truly don't know how lucky we are in this country), mobile phone, crockery and cutlery. So many things that he has taken for granted over the past eighteen years; clean bedding and home-cooked food. He is going to have to sort these out for himself – a steep learning curve then, Steely. Good for the soul or so they say – leaving home and becoming self-sufficient.

It is just impossible to get the vision out of my head of the day we took Cyrus up to Bassingbourn, leaving him on a bench at a bus stop, waiting for a mini bus to whisk him away to a new life. He had whispered under his breath, thinking we hadn't heard, 'What the fuck have I done?' I felt physically sick and we were still about half an hour away from the barracks. He knew deep down that he had made the right decision to join the Army, but the actual cutting of the umbilical cord is painful and tricky for both parent and child, and the reality had finally dawned on him. No hugs or hot chocolate tonight.

Now here we are, saying goodbye to another child – cutting the cord, and praying that goodbye does not mean we'll never see each other again and trying so hard to not make any comparisons – but finding it impossible not to. Could this be the last goodbye too? Stop. I must not live continuously worrying about what might be – but the enormity of letting another son go, and not knowing what the future holds, weighs heavy on me, leaving me tearful and tight-throated.

I worried about Cyrus and how he would cope away from home with people he'd not met before – a strict regime, and physically and mentally hard work. I knew that he would be fed and housed, but the worry about how he would adjust simmered under the surface constantly. Perhaps it was disrespectful, thinking back.

Why would I doubt his ability to survive in the Army? He was tough – he would make it. I knew he would be homesick, as I know that Steely will be homesick – miss his friends, his bed, hot meals, his comfort zone. But I also know that Steely will draw on those reserves of 'tough' that he has, just as Cyrus did. As Cyrus said in his letter, 'Fulfil your dreams.' Somehow this has to be a good moment for us all; Steely moving to America and starting a new life for himself, one he has dreamt of for so many years.

What is it, I wonder, that makes some people feel the need to move away from all they know and have? Both Cyrus and Steely had everything here with us; good friends, freedom, all three of them independent in their own ways. What makes some able to pull away from their lives thus far, and seek different ones? Why has Steely chosen America – why not Brighton, with his college friends? Perhaps America is where he feels the music industry is? I can't put my finger on what it was that made Cyrus join the Army. Possibly the need for adventure, as the challenges are not enough within your normal comfort zone. Does having everything make some (but not all, I know) wish to leave, and go it on your own? In my heart I am sure that they both felt the need for adventure, and some need it more than others. Independence perhaps – that feeling at the end of a life they've yet to experience, that makes them crave the new and unexplored. It's not that I think it is a bad thing – I just wonder what it is that make some able to move away while others stay. That's another thought that keeps me awake at night; the why and wherefores of our children's lives.

Two weeks have flown by, and it's time to have one more hug, stroke his hair one more time, feel his breath on my neck one more time – inhale him. I know I'm working myself up and I need to calm down.

The taxi is here and only three of us get in. I look back and he is walking down the street, pulling his suitcase filled with all the last essentials we could leave; shampoo and deodorant, cans of drink and sachets of hot chocolate. Shoulders square, head high, eyes straight ahead; so like Cyrus in the way he walks. Zac holds my hand all the way to the airport as tears drip silently down my cheeks. Rob sits, ram-rod straight, in the front seat. I'm sure I can hear his heart beating at a gallop. None of us dares look back though, so we just concentrate on breathing. It is all so crushingly sad, watching him disappear over the brow of the hill. When will we see you again, Steely? How long before I can feel the physical pressure of your touch? Don't let me stop you though, my darling, life is to be lived, and this is one of many huge steps you will take without us to hold your hand. I just wish it wasn't so very, very hard to say goodbye.

Two more birthdays celebrated, both in Los Angeles. Another year older, and now they're wiser too, my sons. Men now, no more little boys – men who comfort me and make me stand straight, and not outwardly buckle, which is what I want to do. Weep for boys lost, but take pride in men created.

Thursday and we're home, physically and mentally exhausted; jet-lag is cruel. My head is full of enough confusion without the added displacement that different time-zones bring. Friday, and Ian and Paul Beecroft, the Coroner's Officer, come over at our request, to discuss the procedure we will endure on the following Wednesday. Only back in England six days after having to say goodbye to Steely, and now after sixteen months we will have to face the inquest.

Why has it taken so long? I know that many of the other soldiers who were killed after Cyrus have already had their inquests, so what was the delay with ours? Was there a significant reason, or is it just that we have found ourselves caught up in the court's rota? This uncertainty adds to the pressure bubbling below the surface. It's hard to have a conversation because my mind is distracted, and I'm frightened of what I'm going to hear, of how I'm going to react – of how I'm going to behave.

We are still unsure as to whether we should attend or not. Would it help? Would it erase my nightmares? Would it create new ones? I know it won't change the outcome, so what do we do?

Both Ian and Paul said we could leave the decision right up to the minute that Ian came to collect us and take us to Newbury Town Hall. In all honesty there is no toying with the idea of not going. Of course we must go. We need to see this through, even though there is no 'bitter end', just a bitter taste that nothing can erase.

Paul Beecroft was carrying a large ring-binder which he placed in front of us on the dining room table, that so many months ago had been covered with photographs of the various stages of Cyrus's life. The folder seemed to burn a hole in the glass tabletop – or perhaps it was just a hole in my mind. What was in it? Would there be photographs – ones that captured the last moments of his life?

We were given the opportunity to read all or part of the reports – some graphic, some factual. We declined. What would be the point? The only questions that to my mind needed asking were: 'Was he killed instantly? Did he suffer? Did he realise what had happened, and was he frightened?' I don't know if the answers to those questions lie in that binder; somehow I don't think they do, and perhaps we will never truly know anyway, so those pages will be left unturned by us.

Once again, sleep is impossible. Too many questions, too many visions, too much anxiety. On Wednesday, Ian arrived to drive us to Newbury. The atmosphere in the car was palpable – nerves jangled and I suddenly felt car-sick. I will never get used to being chauffeured; it will always have connotations of dread and fear. Fear of the unknown, fear of the known, fear of not being in control. Control was lost many months ago, and I wonder if it will ever return.

Once again we were surrounded by uniforms, both Army and Royal Air Force. Kind faces, stricken faces – faces that I find hard to place. Everyone was out of context and was nervous and fragile. Sixteen months has been such a long time to wait. Do these men remember exactly, or have their minds shut parts out that are too raw, too dangerous, and too traumatic? They would have to summon up the courage to tell us what happened in those last moments, and we would have to summon up the courage to listen to them speak. I felt very small and not prepared for this in any way. I wondered if I looked as grey as Rob does, as physically sick, as desperately sad. I couldn't help him; I could only hold his hand, stand by him, as he was standing by me, and hope together we could get through this.

We were shown into the inquest room and introduced to Peter Bedford the Coroner, who was seated at the end of the room. There were two rows of wooden seats, and we sat at the front with the witnesses behind us, the press table to the right, and a small table with a jug of water and a glass for the witnesses. I was not sure what I was expecting; large maps, photographs of the area, white-boards and microphones. There were none of these things – only wooden tables and chairs, and silent people gathering themselves, steeling themselves, rehearsing their lines, eyes down, preparing to recount events to us as parents, sharing their sorrow and respect, but unable to offer any respite to our pain.

There was a brief outline on IEDs (improvised explosive devices) and their continuous danger to our troops. I think I heard what was said, but I couldn't really recall all the information. It was not relevant anyway – he's dead and that's all this was really about.

Serjeant Darren Palmer was the first to speak. He sat with his statement in front of him, but he didn't read from it. He spoke quietly, with compassion for us, but with frustration at the situation they had found themselves in while escorting the American bomb-disposal team back towards the FOB. He talked of the dangers, of which they were acutely aware, due to IEDs having been found and detonated just a few short minutes before, and the unusual sight of poppies left on a pile of stones.

Next was Serjeant Leon Smith, who half turned and spoke directly to us, describing the sequence of events, the orders he'd given, the positions people were in. Listening to the softly spoken words, I was transported there – hot, dusty, dangerous. They were full of adrenalin, poised ready for possible attack. While the quad bikes were loaded with the heavy equipment, orders were given, soldiers moving into position, then massive sound, dust, smoke, screaming, shouting, confusion, searching for weapons that had been blown out of hands. Acrid smoke, blood, panic at the realisation Cyrus was dead. What the hell just happened? Is everyone else safe? All rushing over to Cyrus, all instincts on full alert but the need to go to him, help him, get him and the rest of them back to the FOB, and out of any more danger. All these visions in a split second in my mind's eye, like the flashes of strobe lights – minute seconds of clarity even though I wasn't there. Images seared onto my retinas. Leon was still talking and I was aware of the sound but unsure of the words. I was too busy watching – my mind scrolling through those pictures he'd painted.

Corporal Llewellyn Bryan spoke last. He had been the last person to talk to Cyrus, see him blink his eyes; share the last breath of air with him. The horror of everything is still etched into all their eyes, and talking about it, and sharing it with us doesn't help. It only reiterates the facts, and brings their minds rushing back to those last moments. It shows us all how fragile life is, and how a sequence of events can end in such disaster and pain.

How did they cope once back at the FOB? What was the sequence of events, once they were in a relatively safe place? Did they scream and rant and rave? Were they violently sick with fear, anger and post-traumatic adrenalin? Did they feel the burning desire to retaliate – to make the enemy pay for this death? No matter how many years of training, nothing can prepare you for the death of a comrade. No whisky is strong enough to wash away the images, and no words can soothe any more. The taste of death must linger.

They sat and spoke to us quietly, with huge respect and affection for Cyrus. They retold their recollection of events on that dreadful day. There is no closure – no ending to this, no putting it away to collect dust on a shelf in my mind. Closure is simply a word used when nothing is left to be said, uttered by those who can go home to their families and continue with their lives without the gaping hole that we have in ours. It is not meant disrespectfully – simply misused. 'Closure' is for proceedings, not for people. Closure is the ability to forget. None of those who were there that day, and those who knew him that weren't, will ever forget – so closure is not relevant to us.

A series of events, a step in the wrong direction, a war that is still being fought: these are the things that lead to Cyrus's death. No blame – just questions. Who was the man who set this device? Is he a farmer by day and terrorist by night? Has he walked our streets, been educated in our schools and been cared for in our hospitals? Is he dead now, or do we still need to fear him?

In his closing statement Peter Bedford spoke of his respect for all our armed forces, and gave praise to the incredible bravery they showed, and their immense capability in carrying out these tremendously dangerous and stressful jobs. He spoke these words to the attending press, but they were directed at the witnesses who had just shared one of their darkest days, and relived the final moments of a fallen comrade. A verdict of 'unlawfully killed while on active service' was recorded.

This was it, then. The paperwork could be filed and we could all go back to our abnormal lives, try to make sense of what has happened and what we have just heard, then move forward – but towards what?

I'm so tired all the time, tortured by sleep deprivation and the inability to switch my brain off, as if in a caffeine-induced wakefulness. I'm exhausted but unable to shut down. Thoughts and images revolve constantly in my head – thinking, thinking, thinking – trying to assimilate the information, all the time knowing that all the re-living of events won't change the outcome, but unable to fully process the information we've been given. I know too that my nightmares will return with a vengeance, piercing my brain, tormenting me with visions I don't want or need. Madness has returned – the madness of a confused and weary soul, fighting the demons that laugh and tease, and make me question my sanity every day. Does it show, this madness?

How do I stop the vicious circle of self-pity, self-hate, the wish to self-mutilate, and the inability to function as a normal person? I guess I move with it and through it, allowing it to push me along.

Rob had asked for the GPS co-ordinates of Cyrus's last breath. These we received a few days after the inquest. They too sit in the chest in the front room, slowly burning a hole in our beings.

If we so wished to, when Afghanistan is finally free of war and terror, I wonder if we would visit this place? Step on the dusty track, touch the earth, breathe the air. Would going there make us become a part of what Cyrus was trying to achieve by being a soldier? Could this give us something positive or would it mock our stupidity and romantic ideas about any achievements that had been made in his, and so many other people's names? Would we go hoping this spot would or could offer us something? I think like the memorials and headstone, it will only give sadness and sorrow. All it would do would be to transfer those feelings to the side of a dusty track in a far off land that only holds pain for us, not hope.

We left the Town Hall after the inquest and moved towards the waiting press. We'd prepared a speech beforehand, together with copies, so no awkward questions could be asked. The inquest was over, this stage complete. The facts had been established, accounts pieced together to create a picture. A few words now for those interested enough to read them, then home, having said goodbye to Leon and the others. I wonder when, or if, we will see them again.

> *'Today has been a difficult day. A day we've known we would have to face, and it has proved to be as hard as we imagined but we decided that we would not shy away and that we were going to stand proud and be brave for Cyrus in all aspects of his life and his tragic death last year.*
>
> *For us as a family, the past sixteen months have been horrendous and before Cyrus's death it was beyond imagination that it was possible to*

*feel as sad as we do and we simply can't see the
next sixteen months being any easier.'*

Everyone melted away, and I was left with the feeling of emptiness again – the end of one part of our lives but the beginning of the next, knowing nothing could ever be the same again for anyone who has been part of Cyrus's life.

CHAPTER 16

ONCE MORE POPPIES AND PAIN

Here we are again – November and all that goes with that month. I've started to wear my poppy pin. Steely has been in Los Angeles for six weeks now. I miss him, Rob misses him, and Zac misses him. The house feels empty, and yet there are still three of us here, moving around each other, touching sometimes and repelling others, like magnets. There is nothing bad in needing our own space and time to be with our own thoughts, but it is comforting to know we are here for each other.

Gun-metal grey: how ironic that that's the colour of the sky today. The leaves are turning – but not as quickly as I remember in the past, or perhaps I don't remember things as clearly any more. Grey, damp, windy November – not the nicest of months anyway, but now the malice of dying leaves and withered flowers touches where it went unnoticed before.

A week of engagements, all meant for the best, but all so difficult to carry out without feeling the need to tear my hair out. Putting on our brave faces as people want to see a positive; they can cope with that, while negativity is too destructive and personal.

Chiltern Edge School have raised over £1,000 for 2 Rifles – fantastic – so Rob and I went and collect the cheque, tell them what Remembrance Day means to us and let them know who will benefit from their efforts. I'm not sure they really understand; the only way is to have experienced our loss, and we wouldn't wish that on them.

Wednesday brought something new: the March for Honour, which has been organised by Lance Corporal Ram Pattern of the Royal Marines, with members from all of the forces marching a mile for each fallen solider from Iraq and Afghanistan since operations began in 2001. He decided he wanted to do something to raise awareness, so the plan to do this sponsored speed-march began.

We met at the Civic Centre in Reading, together with the Lord Lieutenant, several Mayors, the press and, of course, the British Legion. We joined Ram and walked through Broad Street, cheered by shoppers and on-lookers, and met up with others at the Memorial in Forbury Gardens. Eileen Green (Richard's mother) was there together with Claire, his stepmother. We had been given a wreath by the Legion and Rob, Eileen and I stepped up and placed in on the memorial.

No amount of support or the laying of wreaths makes any of this better. I wish it were that simple, but it is important to keep their memories alive this way, and also to see the support that there is out there for our forces, and for us.

Thursday was Remembrance Day, and we'd been asked by the Reverend of Shiplake College to come and join them for their Remembrance Service, and give a short talk on why we felt Remembrance Day was important. Strange to be asked by the College, as this was who Zac went to Kenya with, and yet the Reverend knew nothing of that connection until we pointed it out over coffee after the service.

It was daunting to stand in front of upwards of two hundred people and talk about anything, let alone about Remembrance Day and Cyrus. I felt that we managed to give them an understanding of what wars mean to those that have lost a loved one. Cyrus was seventeen when he joined up, and several of them in the congregation were that age. It's all very well talking about the Great Wars, but none of us remembers them, even if we were affected indirectly. This war is so much more available – if that's the right way of describing it. The internet, the instant news, and mobile phones make this an accessible war – one that we can watch from the comfort of our living rooms. So I tried to explain why it is a war that affects us all today, rather than expecting them to equate themselves to those grainy black and white photos of the hell that was WWI and WWII.

Rob and I went up to Cyrus's grave for 11 o'clock, and Chris and Claire Green were there for Richard. Chilly (Rob's most supportive friend) came too, five of us all locked in our own grief. Our thoughts are also with someone else today – Joan Walkling, a little old lady for whom Rob had done odd-jobs and known for over thirty years. She died yesterday after battling cancer for more than five years. She was in her eighties and always used to say she knew she'd had a 'good innings', but nevertheless her death was very sad. She had become a huge part of our lives. Zac, Cyrus and Steely had become her surrogate grandchildren and she their surrogate grandmother.

Over the years she had become very dependent on Rob, as even changing light-bulbs and batteries in a bedside clock were tasks she struggled with. She had been a huge support to Rob over the last eighteen months, and they would have done anything for each other. Rob had been to see her at the hospice at 9 o'clock the morning before, and later received a phone call with the news that she had died that lunchtime. He will miss her – she was a true friend.

On Friday we went to Micklands Primary School once again for their assembly, which was given by Ian Tindall about 'The Poppy'. Listening to Ian talk, I'd not known about half of the things that he told them, but one thing that really struck me was that 1964 is the only year since the end of WWII that no forces were killed on active duty. It now made sense of those sixteen thousand plus names on the memorial at The National Arboretum. How many pebbles thrown into millponds whose ripples have been felt all over the world?

There had been a change of plan for Remembrance Sunday. The Regiment were sending Elliott and Malou over to represent 2 Rifles, and several representatives from 3 Rifles were going to be there for Richard, together with two buglers. I called the Caversham branch of the Legion and explained that we'd not be down at the river with them at the War Memorial, so asked them to please send our apologies to everyone who attended their service. They had been so kind getting Cyrus's name engraved, and we felt it right to let them know why we wouldn't be there.

Elliott had arrived on Saturday, driven from London by his mother, and we asked her in to have a cup of tea. It was very hard to watch her as she talked about how he was struggling to come to terms with everything. He would be leaving the Army in January. He had also had another blow – in the early hours of Friday morning two of his friends from school were killed in a car accident. Fucking hell, how much more? There is just nothing I can say.

Zac and Elliott went out for the evening, and eventually crawled into their beds at 5 am – not much time to sleep before we had to be at graveside. Malou arrived to a cup of tea and a bacon sandwich, and my mother arrived too, bringing with her crosses and a wreath from herself and Mione's family.

Rob and I had already decided that, as we weren't quite sure how the whole thing was going to work, I would (with the permission of Richard's family) say a few words and read the Rifleman's Collect just before 11 am, which would be followed by two minutes' silence and the sounding of the Last Post and Reveille. I stood between their headstones and read – it was one of the hardest things I've had to do. It's the 'Swift and Bold' that always gets me and then those clear haunting notes from the bugle. Even after hearing it several times the feeling of utter desperation still closes in on me, making it difficult to breathe and concentrate.

We laid wreaths, two families and friends wrapped up against the cold and wrapped up in grief. The

Sambuca made an appearance; everyone had a little sip and privately toasted our boys.

Pete Bevan turned up in motorbike leathers with a wreath. Such a nice man, he was a Corporal when he trained Cyrus in Bassingbourn. I don't know if Pete has lost anyone else he knows in this war, but it was very kind of him to come for Cyrus and to show his support for us. He came back home with us and had a cup of tea before braving the rain and heading back to Abingdon, where he is now stationed. It still surprises me how many people Cyrus touched in his life, and how many people miss him.

So that's it. Another Remembrance Week come and gone. Exhaustion overwhelms me but sleep is still as evasive as ever, ruined by dreams and a mind that refuses to shut down. Christmas next, I guess. I've already planned that we won't have a tree again; too many memories associated with that ritual, too painful to do, sorry boys – I hope you'll understand.

People often ask me how I am and that they can't imagine how I feel. How to describe it? I never sleep through a whole night any more, and when I do sleep I wake in an instant, no warm gentle sleepy awakening, but a sudden heart-stopping wake when I know in a split second that it's all true. The feeling is almost a hunger, gnawing in the pit of my stomach like stage fright; that butterfly kiss that is so cruel. That moment when my heart breaks all over again. That is what it feels like, all day and every day, with no change over the days and months – no peace, only deep sorrow and the huge feeling of loss that no food, drink or medicine can ever heal. It's a wound carved into my very being. This is how

I feel, so how do I break that to the person asking such a question, without making them feel embarrassed that they asked it in the first place?

In reality, I'd like to tell them to imagine someone who is nearest and dearest to them, and out of the blue they are told that person has been blown to pieces. For an instant this may give them an understanding, but the truth is they will have forgotten that feeling by the time the conversation is over. The difference between us is I am reminded of this every time my brain thinks it can relax for a moment. But I know that's not what they want to hear, so I just smile and say I'm getting there or I'm ok. But that is just a lie, like my make-up.

CHAPTER 17

THE SECOND CHRISTMAS

Fewer cards have dropped on to the mat this year, perhaps because I've not been able to send any myself, who knows? I don't really care, but the question lingers. I guess people don't know what to say that they haven't said already, heartfelt words that fall on a wounded soul, words that are unable to comfort or bring peace and that's what Christmas is all about, peace and harmony I've none of those things any more.

Steely is due home on 22nd December and we are so looking forward to him being back, even though it's only for a few days. He will breathe fresh air into our lives again, be able to share his adventures, and tell us about his life in LA. I can't wait.

I've not been into Reading to shop. I can't face it – too many people smiling, laughing and jostling each other with their bags and tubes of wrapping paper. I'm not brave enough yet, so the boys will have to have things bought via the internet or the supermarket.

It's snowing, cold and icy and travel is getting harder. I have that underlying feeling of dread. I daren't say it out loud in case it comes true, but I have a terrible feeling that flights are going to start being cancelled. Stay positive, don't worry – it will be fine.

Seven o'clock on the morning of 21st December and the internet is screaming at me the words I had so dreaded. Flight VS008 from Los Angeles *cancelled*. This simply can't be true. Surely we are due some luck this time. No.

I'd not realised how vulnerable we all still are. 'Gutted' is the only way I can describe it. The worst news we'd heard for over a year. How can this possibly be happening to us? He still doesn't know – they are eight hours behind us. All day we have to live with the knowledge that we have to ring him and tell him he can't come home. It's been a black day, my eyes are red from crying and I feel sick all the time. Ridiculous – I know he is well, he is safe, he is alive – but not going to be here with us. All the feelings of panic and the inability to function properly return with a vengeance. It's hard to breathe, my chest tightens and nothing is in focus. How can I be feeling this all over again? The news is almost as devastating as if we'd been told he too had been killed. So much hope had been pinned on him coming home. We've soured over the months and he would have been there to sweeten us all again.

Rob rings him. There is a silence and all I hear is Rob asking, 'Are you still there, mate?' Oh God, why this pain all the time? Why do we have to be breaking bad news to our children again? 'I'm here Dad, it's ok, I just needed to take it all in really.' He's so brave and adult about it.

He's comforting us – surely that's all back-to-front? He the parent and we the devastated and disappointed children, how odd.

He's ok. We're not. Now Christmas without two of my boys. We Skyped him and he sat on the end of the table, framed by a computer screen while we opened our presents. It was lovely to see him – Skype... what a magic invention. Seeing his face made it all seem less dark. He reminds me of Cyrus in so many ways, all three of them had/have something in common – a bravery that runs through their very beings. I wish I had some of it. I'm not brave, I just feel old and terribly, terribly sad.

We made it through, but it wasn't the same. It will never be the same again and I knew that last year. I guess I hoped it would be easier this year – but how stupid am I?

Once again I find myself teetering on the edge of insanity, feeling the need to metaphorically slit my wrists, peel back the flesh and rid myself of the pain that lives under my skin. The inky blackness of night consumes me during the day – that 'full moon' feeling that never strays far from my conscious thoughts. I've tried to rationalise it, put myself into a 'category' to reason my way out, but those are tools used by counsellors who think that we are all basically the same creature, who can be reached and healed with words that are hollow and meaningless. I've lost my future and my past, my meaning and my children. My children disappeared on 2nd June 2009. They became adults out of necessity – the need to survive, the need to cope – and the innocence of childhood became a distant memory. We all lost our past that day. The memories are still there but the ability to see them clearly has gone; they are defused with pain and sorrow, they are opaque, rather than crystal clear. That is why we have lost our past.

My life is not a corridor whose path has been blocked. There is no 'other' way around that blockage. I had a life – we all did – and now that life has gone. It's not hidden or been moved – it has simply gone. Snuffed out, stolen. There are no soothing words, no book, no recipe for 'better'; there is a new life needing to be learned, new paths to be woven into the fabric of our souls. Different, and at times hateful – a life I don't want but have to take. There is no choice that isn't a completely selfish one and I still have no desire to take that option.

2011. I wonder what this year will bring. Last year was a blur, and looking back I can't really remember anything in great detail. Strange, as I thought that I was less blank than I had been the previous year. Odd, how we move through our spaces in life, not really taking it all in, and yet living as though we are; going through the motions of living, but not living. Surely to have a life you have to appreciate it – or at least take part in it. I don't feel as though I've been able to do that these past months. I wonder if this will change with time, and whether or not I will continue to merely exist rather than live.

13th January: Cyrus would have been twenty-one today. There is a balloon announcing it on his grave – a gesture made full of good intentions and love but excruciatingly painful to see, bobbing almost joyfully in the wind. How dare it? Rob untied it, releasing it to the wind and we watched as it disappeared into the distance. It seemed symbolic somehow. I miss him so very much every second, minute, hour, day, month, year – every birthday and forever more.

The past is hard to conjure up sometimes, but it is my past, shared with Rob, Zac, Cyrus and Steely. It is who I am, why I am the person I am, what makes me strive, even through this awfulness, to continue to be who I am. Cyrus was a huge part of everything we are, and without him I wonder, would we have had the great times we did. He, as part of my family, has given me some of the best years of my life – times of laughter, peace, love, joy and pride. The pride of seeing him join the Army, taking that vow, Passing Off after a long physically and mentally hard period of basic training, and becoming a man. Without him in my life I wonder if I would be able to say that I have truly experienced everything that this life can throw at me. He has left a huge hole in our lives, but we will continue to love and support each other, move forward – knowing that it is exactly what he would have expected of us. It would be so disrespectful of me to just give up – he would never have given up on anything in his life, and I intend to honour his memory by being the best person I can, despite this massive mountain I have to climb.

When Cyrus was in Year 8 he wrote a poem, and I came across it again recently as I was looking through some paperwork. It was part of some things that the staff at his school had found and put to one side for us. The words are those of a young boy not knowing what he wanted to do with his life or what road it would take. It is completely ironic.

I'm on a Kamikaze mission, so follow no laws,
I can be big and dangerous but have no jaws.

I'm sometimes bright colours, pink purple and red
But if you touch me, I will steal your leg.

I can be hidden in fields, jungles and such
There are thousands of me, I don't cost much.

My life is dedicated to terror and fear,
I rip through the flesh of those who come near.

It's not only people, animals as well.
My purpose in life is to make your life hell.

To rid this world of me and my friends,
Would take years and months, days upon end.

The life I live has a very long line,
In case you've not guessed, I am a landmine.

Cyrus Thatcher 8LC

Oh Cyrus, I love you my darling. I wish I could tell you. I wish I could hold you. I wish you were here. **Mum x**

SSAFA FORCES Help

The death of a family member, especially while still young, changes everything. We each cope with loss in a different way, but it can help to share feelings with someone who has been through a similar experience.

The Soldiers, Sailors, Airmen and Families Association (SSAFA) Forces Help is an established military charity that takes care of those currently serving, their families and veterans. As an increasing number of British troops became casualties of the recent conflicts in Afghanistan and Iraq it became clear that the families of those who had died needed and deserved additional support.

The death of a son or daughter can only be truly understood by those who have experienced it. The SSAFA Bereaved Families Support Group was established by families themselves and helps whether a death occurred in a combat or non-combat situation. From coping with emotional turmoil to the practicalities of dealing with the MoD and inquests. Those who have recently suffered loss are able to gain strength and knowledge from those further along the path.

The families meet around the UK with special support groups available for the siblings of those who have been killed. A similar mutual support group operates for those families where someone has suffered a serious life-changing injury.

For further information regarding SSAFA Forces Help and the Support Groups visit **www.ssafasupportgroups.org.uk** or call **0845 1300 975**.

FireStep
Publishing

FireStep Publishing is a new division of military book specialists *Tommies Guides*, first established in 2005 by Ryan Gearing. Our aim is to publish up to 100 books and related product a year and bring new and old titles alive for the military enthusiast whilst having the ability and desire through many of our book projects to work with and to support HM Forces and related charities.

We offer an unparalleled range of services from traditional publishing through to assisted self-publishing and bespoke packages for the discerning and specialist author, historian, genealogist, museum or organisation. We are always looking for new ideas and ventures and especially welcome enquiries from military museums and organisations with a view to partnering in publishing projects.

We pride ourselves on our commitment to each book and our authors, our professionalism and being able to work solely within the military genre, with the knowledge, contacts and expertise to maximise the potential of any of our products.

For more information on any of our titles, to contact us with suggestions for new books, or just to keep in touch with our latest news and products, please visit our website: www.firesteppublishing.com